THE SCHOOL
THAT
FELL FROM THE SKY

THE SCHOOL
THAT
FELL FROM THE SKY

BY

FRED HARGESHEIMER

eBookstand Books

Published by
eBookstand Books
Division of the Magnum Group
Auburn, CA 95604

ISBN 1-58909-116-7

Printed in the United States of America

For DOROTHY, my beloved wife
and favorite bridge partner

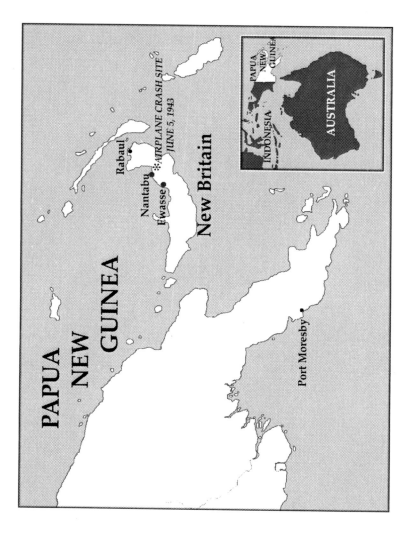

PAPUA NEW GUINEA

Rabaul

AIRPLANE CRASH SITE
JUNE 5, 1943

Nantabu
Ewasse

New Britain

Port Moresby

PAPUA NEW GUINEA

INDONESIA

AUSTRALIA

PREFACE

It's now more than forty years since I met Fred Harge-sheimer, but I recall that my first reaction was that he was not only a very good story but also "a helluva good bloke." The smiling, cheerful Fred had just arrived in Papua New Guinea from his home in White Bear Lake, Minnesota, to search out and thank the people of a small village deep in the jungle of rugged New Britain for having saved his life in wartime 1943.

I was then the editor of the Sydney-based *Pacific Islands Monthly*, and New Guinea was a part of my beat, so naturally I was keen to report the story of this American airman whose P-38 had been shot down, and who had managed, though injured, to bail out over that Japanese-occupied island. Alone, and not sure just where he was, he had survived for a month on bamboo shoots, snails, and a couple of chocolate bars before being seen by people from Nantabu village, who hid him from searching Japanese patrols and nursed him back to health. By this time, back at the squadron, Fred had long been given up for dead. The villagers succored him for five months, eventually connecting him up with a small party of Australian military Coastwatchers who had been landed on New Britain to report enemy movements. Fred himself became an active Coastwatcher before being taken out by submarine another three months later.

So he had come back to thank the villagers. But as good a story as it was then, it got even better after Fred went back to Minnesota, for he was determined to do something substantial for them. We followed him up, and in occasional reports in our pages over many years Fred became admired, as he is still admired on my side of the Pacific, as the American who wouldn't forget, who decided to build a school for the people in that remote area of New Britain, who established a foundation and raised the funds for the school, the man who built it and got it staffed.

In those early years he worked on it with his own hands, with the help of his warm and supportive wife Dorothy and one of their sons, Dick. They built it at Ewasse, not far from Nantabu but more accessible for the region, and named it the Airmen's Memorial School. Fred and Dorothy lived among the villagers for some years, two well-balanced people doing a job on the other side of the world because they decided it needed doing. I know of no greater story of dedication in the Pacific, dedication done so cheerfully, than the story of Fred Hargesheimer and his family.

Fred tells his story in these pages. It's a great read, and even all these years later I choked up at the detailed account of his wartime experiences on New Britain, although I thought I knew them. Fred's recollections about what the people did for him are so vivid and honest that he makes it easier for us to see why, as he says, he "*had* to go back." But Fred of course not only went back, he has kept on going back, and he rather too modestly avoids telling us the details of the difficulties he has faced and overcome over the years in developing a very successful school and its many parts. Many of the problems of course were thrown up by the sheer distance and communication problems between New Britain and the United States. But Fred is there for the long haul. His more than forty years of work and dedication are a triumph of faith, perseverance, and humanity.

Stuart Inder,
Sydney, Australia
May 2002

ACKNOWLEDGEMENTS

To my children—Dick, Eric, and Carol—for their patience and support.

To my Nakanai friends—Luluai Lauo; Joseph Gabu; Ida and Apelis Tagogo, and many others—first for saving my life, second for working with me on our common goal of the school, and finally for inspiring me to put my story into print.

To the friends who have provided help and hospitality during my visits to Papua New Guinea: Garua and Ekonia Peni; Merv and Ishka King; Bet Whitten; Ray Thurecht; Bill and Ruth Townsend; Freddie and June Kaad; Dougal and Debbie Geddes; Matt Foley; Don and Annette Marshall; Robin and Phyllis Jayesuria; Stuart and Jo Inder; Jim and Marilyn Bye; and many more.

To attorney Les Mikeworth, who prepared (*pro bono)* the legal documents establishing the Airmen's Nantabu Memorial Foundation as a non-profit organization.

To the overseas volunteer teachers: Linda Clerc and Charlie Parfrey; Ann and Jerry Parks; and Rick Chandler.

To the Royal Air Force Escaping Society, the Fred P. Archer Charitable Trust, and everyone else who has given time and/or money to the Airmen's Memorial Schools.

To writers Ursa Heinz and Curtis Haynes for their collaborative support; to Gregg Schiffner for the cover design; to Stuart Inder and Susan Heiden for their helpful feedback; and a special thanks to my copy editor Judy Patton for the hours of discussion over coffee at Hollywood Sweets and the many subsequent hours of work required to make the manuscript fit for printing.

THE ADVENTURE BEGINS

It was early evening on May 7, 1916. Oscar Hargesheimer and Doc Crewe were planning their next fishing trip as they lingered over coffee at the Hargesheimer's kitchen table in Rochester, Minnesota. Oscar's wife Lucy was making the cake for which she was famous—a rich and chocolaty devil's food.

When the batter was finished she spooned it into the tins, put them into the oven, snapped the oven door shut, and turned to the men, saying, "I think it's time, Oscar."

The trio went upstairs. Fifteen minutes later Lucy delivered into Doc Crewe's waiting hands a third son, Fred. Holding me up by the heels, he spanked my bottom and I took my first breath.

The word *adventure* comes from a Latin root meaning "arrival," but almost any adventure entails a going out. With that first breath my adventure began. My older brothers were Walter and Richard. Robert and Mary Louise came after me. It was my good fortune to get launched into a close-knit family headed by loving parents. They gave us strong values and taught us self-reliance and a can-do attitude. They did it all without raising their voices in anger, but I imagine that five lively children provided them with plenty of reasons to do otherwise.

Stories of the early days were part of our heritage. My mother came along in 1886, the third of eight children born to Harvey and Mary Gould Durkee in Charles City, Iowa. Grandpa Durkee was a schoolteacher, which didn't impress us nearly as much as the rumor that he had been a drummer boy for General Grant's troops during the Civil War. Somewhere along the way he mastered the art of Spenserian penmanship, a skill much admired in that era. He earned pocket money by lettering business cards for traveling salesmen, and was greatly honored to do the invitations for President Arthur's inauguration. John Soule's exhortation to "go West, young man" obviously appealed to him, for he eventually moved to Southern California, where he published a newspaper and established a real-estate business.

When Congress passed the Homestead Act in 1909, the Durkee adventuresome spirit prompted my mother and her older sister Mable to take advantage of the opportunity to acquire free land. The two girls joined the land rush to South Dakota, where each was granted a quarter-section of prairie land near the settlement of Philip. All they had to do to "prove up the claims" was pay a

1

sixteen-dollar fee and pass an inspection to verify that the property had been under cultivation for fifteen months.

My mother Lucy was just eighteen years old. Except for her sister, the nearest neighbor was five miles away. Surely their parents must have been generous with their aid, for they had small wood-framed houses, barns and privies, horses and equipment. During the harsh winters, blowing snow often reduced visibility to near zero. Ropes strung between the buildings were literally lifelines.

In addition to frigid winters and hot dry summers, Lucy and Mable soon learned that isolation was another challenge to cope with. The all-day trip to Phillips provided them with more than just supplies; it gave them a chance to socialize as well. During the winter months they hitched their horses to a sleigh, put heated bricks underneath their feet, and piled on blankets to stave off the cold. Lucky were the ones who possessed buffalo robes! The travelers were fortified by the knowledge that at the end of their journey they would find people, conversation, and news—not to mention music and dancing!

Those dances were of necessity all-night affairs because it was too dangerous to ride back home in the dark without marked roads. The young families brought their children, and when sleep overtook the little ones they were bedded down with blankets in some out-of-the-way corner. The adults kicked up their heels until they or the musicians grew tired. Morning meant they had to endure the long trip home, but along with their supplies they brought back many happy memories.

My father, Oscar Hargesheimer, was born in Rochester, Minnesota on November 17, 1880. He followed family tradition and became a pharmacist, as had his father and his older brothers Gus and Max. In 1898, shortly after his father died, he left school and began working at the family drugstore. Under the tutelage of one or the other of his brothers, he became what was laughingly called a pill roller. In those days pharmacists actually made many of the pills they dispensed by grinding up crude medicines with a mortar and pestle, adding the proper amount of moisture, and rolling the resulting "dough" into pills. (For this reason the mortar and pestle was a familiar logo on the signs that hung in front of pharmacies.) They also made their own infusions and tinctures from the raw drugs. Some were added to syrups flavored with peppermint, wintergreen, or anise to make them more palatable.

2

Pop told of getting to work at six-thirty in the morning, before the mail went out on the routes. I gathered from his accounts that they mailed medicines to those customers who found the trip into town too difficult. The pharmacy apprentices put in long hours, often working and studying until ten or eleven at night. There was no time to fool around, scarcely time to eat and sleep.

After passing the state board examination and getting his pharmacist's certificate, Pop went to Wyckoff, Minnesota, where he operated a drugstore from 1902 until 1906.

In 1906, attracted by the promise of greater opportunities, Pop decided to go west. He settled in Philip, South Dakota, where he started another drugstore (keeping the one in Wyckoff as well). Being an enterprising young man, he took advantage of the new Homestead Act and took up a claim on an eighty-acre parcel.

From 1908 to 1912 the area around Philip suffered a severe drought. For four years there were practically no crops, hence no money for people to spend. During that time Pop became enamored with a young lady from Iowa, and on September 4, 1911 he married Miss Lucy Durkee. A year later they left Philip and moved back to Rochester.

Pop was an outstanding fisherman. The younger folks always considered it an honor to join him on a fishing trip. Minnesota, with its many streams and lakes, is a fisherman's paradise. My memories include the many times Pop would come home with a creel full of freshly caught trout. As he cleaned them he would examine their entrails to see what they had been feeding on. That way, he knew what to use for bait at different times of the summer.

Pop did not attend church on a regular basis. We used to jokingly call him a "two-timer" because he never missed the Christmas and Easter services. His true religious observance was the way he lived his life and ran his business. He was a most kind and generous person. The safe in the back of the drugstore held a stack of checks that had been returned by the bank, marked insufficient funds. He obviously believed that the bad-check writers had no intention of cheating him but were simply short of money, so he ignored their debts as a way to help them out.

At Christmastime, as in most households with children, anticipation and excitement reigned. Many preparations went on behind the scenes, most of them orchestrated by our mother. And it didn't take the older children long to figure out that Pop was the one who put the wheel toys together late on Christmas Eve. We were sent off to bed at the usual hour and I don't remember much protesting. The sooner we slept, the sooner the morn. It was our custom to set the alarm to awaken us long before dawn, but that didn't mean we could rush downstairs willy-nilly and begin opening packages. There was a ritual to be followed in the Hargesheimer household. First we had to line up in front of the bathroom door according to age and take care of our morning ablutions. Once we were dressed and groomed, we gathered in the same order at the head of the stairs and waited for Santa (Pop of course). When his "Ho! Ho! Ho!" and the jingling of bells echoed up the stairway, we clattered down en mass.

Some years after the advent of prohibition, a figurative black mark appeared on the Hargesheimer calendar. When the town's duck hunters were out in their freezing blinds complaining that they would surely die of hypothermia or pneumonia without their usual belly-warming nips, Dr. Crewe neatly solved the problem. Leaving the spaces for the patients' names blank, he wrote out a stack of prescriptions for medicinal whiskey and handed them to my father. As medical needs arose before each hunting trip, Pop filled in the names and dispensed the prescribed cure—one pint of bonded bourbon. The hunters stayed happy and healthy.

Pop was the one who wound up in the cooler. One day the Feds showed up at the pharmacy door, chained it shut, and took him into custody. Judge Irving Eckholdt, who heard the case, was my father's fishing buddy, but the law was the law, and Pop was sent off to the Wabasha prison on the banks of the Mississippi River.

The warden came to enjoy Pop's company and soon made him a "trusty" (a trustworthy inmate who was granted special privileges and responsibilities). On quiet days they headed out to the river together for a few hours of fishing. On weekends Mom would pack a picnic basket and, since she didn't drive, I was most happy to show off my skills by driving her to the prison. She and Pop would share the contents of the hamper while the warden's daughter Barbara and I spent a happy afternoon cruising the river on the Delta Queen, a paddle-wheel steamer. Those prison picnics relieved the tedium of my father's incarceration and were a pleasant interlude for both of my parents.

While Pop paid the price for circumventing the law, he never thought of himself as a criminal—and he wasn't viewed as such. Mom, however, felt that the Hargesheimer reputation was forever besmirched. She was a very small person, but large in grit and determination. She could be up to her ears in problems that would have seemed insurmountable to someone else, but she responded by holding her head high and going about the business of daily living.

Many others found themselves in my father's predicament. These men were not at all in the same category as the speakeasy operators, rumrunners, and purveyors of bathtub gin who flourished during the prohibition years and were the source of gang wars and unspeakable crimes.

While Pop was incarcerated, the two licensed pharmacists who worked at the drugstore carried on the business. Mom relayed instructions from my father and kept the young men on their toes. She could be a diligent taskmaster.

The Hargesheimer home was on the side of what was known as "pill hill" because the residents represented a cross-section of the medical profession. There was even a Nobel-Prize winner among them. Our two-story white stucco house boasted a basement, an attic, and a two-car garage. It cost six thousand dollars when it was built in 1916. The basement was dominated by a coal-fired furnace. We boys were responsible for removing the ashes; in the wintertime we spread them on the driveway to provide traction. The basement also featured a Maytag washing machine with a hand-operated wringer, as well as a two-burner gas plate where a copper tub could be placed for boiling white clothes. We also had a mangle—a revolving drum with a gas burner inside—to make lighter work of ironing sheets and the many shirts worn by the male members of the household.

At one end of the basement we had a basketball hoop, which, although not of regulation height, served us well and provided a good place to play during inclement weather.

It must have been about 1928 when Pop decided to add a restaurant to the pharmacy. He had enough tables to seat forty-five, along with a small counter. That's when the basement was altered to house a bakery. Mom took on the task of baking pies and cakes, with her devil's food at the top of the list. Six days a week she and a helper toiled down there. The smell of all those goodies probably drove the neighbors crazy.

The attic was also well utilized. With a mat on the floor it became a wrestling arena. With music racks it became a practice room for a drummer and a horn tooter. (I'm sure our parents appreciated the insulating space between them and the living quarters.) We even did our homework up there. And we had a large second-floor porch that was eventually made into a boys' dormitory.

We were happy to have our own digs, so we didn't begrudge Mary Louise her private room.

Such a large home required a lot of care. We had a lovely live-in maid named Lillian Antonson who was viewed as part of the family. She was paid twelve dollars a week and of course had her own room.

Strangely enough, the fact that we had only one bathroom was not unusual for those times. Managing to make ourselves presentable, eat breakfast, and walk a mile to school without being late was a daily miracle. Our milk—whole, rich, and unpasteurized—came from Guernsey cows and was delivered in glass bottles. The cream rose to the top, of course, and was probably one of the reasons we hurried through our morning ablutions: the early birds got cream on their cereal!

Many of the things we looked upon as conveniences would seem terribly old-fashioned today. In the basement we had a concrete cistern that collected rainwater runoff from the roof. A hand pump mounted at the kitchen sink was a wonderful source for soft water, which was much prized (especially by the women) for shampooing hair.

Household refrigeration was not readily available in the early years, so in the summertime we relied on a wooden icebox that held a fifty-pound chunk of ice. It came with a color-coded cardboard square marked with the various sizes of ice available. We placed the square in a front window with the number fifty at the top so the iceman could see it as he cruised the neighborhood. He came three times a week and usually had a flock of kids trailing along behind him. They weren't there to keep him company; they hoped to be recipients of any ice chips that happened to fall to the side. The iceman used a pick to divide the huge chunks he brought from the ice plant. It was amazing how he could follow an imaginary line across the top of a piece of ice and suddenly it would cleanly separate into the desired sizes.

We could always find something to occupy ourselves. During the summer we made our own fun and often hiked out to our favorite swimming hole on the Zumbro River. I don't think Mom worried about us. There was usually a bunch of kids out there, escaping the heat, so we weren't alone. We soon learned to swim like fish.

Sandlot baseball was another pastime. There were no organizations such as Babe Ruth, Little League, or Junior Legion to provide uniforms, equipment, coaches, and umpires for us. We

6

improvised, marking out the diamond by drawing lines in the sand with a stick. Bases were squares of old carpet, and since we seldom had two full sets of gear, the teams shared whatever was available. Players took turns being the umpire. Parents rarely showed up, and those who did either sat in their cars or cheered from the sidelines.

In the wintertime we rode our toboggans and Flexible Flyer sleds down the steep hillside in front of our house. Sometimes a friendly neighbor would put chains on his car, hitch up a bunch of sleds, and tow us to the top. One cold Saturday a trip down that icy hill nearly ended in tragedy for my brother Bob. About halfway down he lost control and sped across the rutted snow, ending up a crumpled heap at the foot of a telephone pole. He came running into the house with a bloody nose and a mouthful of broken teeth. Fortunately Dr. Louis Austin, a dental surgeon who lived next door, had come home from the Mayo Clinic for lunch. My sister ran to tell him of the accident. Bob had to hang his head over the kitchen sink while Dr. Louis removed the teeth that dangled by their roots.

That accident made Bob a neighborhood hero of sorts, for he had survived what each of us dreaded but never voiced. Flying down that hill was an exhilarating experience, but fear always rode on our shoulders—fear that what had happened to Bob, or something even worse, might happen to us. The smiles that shone on our faces after a successful trip to the bottom were expressions of joy mixed with triumph.

On the whole we were a healthy bunch of kids. I suppose we had the usual childhood bouts with measles, mumps, and whooping cough. I know we got vaccinations, because they left their marks on every arm. And one experience permanently left its mark on my memory. For some reason, when I was ten years old, it was decided that my tonsils should be removed. The deed was done not at the hospital but in Dr. Crewe's office, which was located above my father's pharmacy. Early one morning I found myself on a gurney in what passed for a surgery. Pop was the anesthesiologist. Under Dr. Crewe's direction, he dripped ether on the cone slapped over my nose and told me to take deep breaths. I did as I was told and that's the last thing I remember. When I came to, my stomach lurched with nausea and my throat hurt like the very devil. When I had recovered enough to hold my head up, I was escorted on rubbery legs out to the car and taken home.

I curled up on the davenport, completely miserable. Misery piled upon misery when I learned that the rest of the family was in the dining room eating pancakes covered with real maple syrup, my favorite food. Oh the injustice of it all! If only their breakfast had been oatmeal—that wouldn't have seemed so bad.

Since my mother wasn't interested in learning to drive a car, getting away from home any distance at all was a matter of walking, hitchhiking, or riding a bike. There was just one bicycle for the five of us. We knew we'd better not squabble over it or it wouldn't be available to any of us. As a result, we learned to negotiate.

Seventh grade marked the point at which we joined the big kids at Rochester's combination junior and senior high school. I finished sixth grade at the age of ten, so I was just a little kid mixed in with those hulking teenagers. Farm kids were brought in by bus and brown-bagged their lunches, but we city kids had to walk home—in our case a mile. We had just an hour to race home, eat lunch, and get back to school. Needless to say there were no lagging appetites.

Miss Whiting, principal of junior high, was a strict disciplinarian who kept us in line. She prepared us well for the time when we would be under the eagle eye of Belva Snodgrass, principal of senior high. A large lady with piercing eyes and an equally sharp tongue, Miss Snodgrass could turn a varsity football player into a wimp. Word of her filtered down to the lowliest of us.

Under that same roof, up on the fourth floor, junior college classes were held, making it easy for many of us to have a go at further education.

Our family was active in high-school sports. Walt and Rich both played on the varsity football and basketball teams. Walt was captain of the basketball team in his senior year, and later played second-string quarterback for Bernie Berman on the University of Minnesota's national championship team. One year he and his partner won the Big-Ten tennis doubles championship.

Bob and I looked up to our older brothers and hoped to do as well. I opted to go out for swimming and tennis, which, although not contact sports, were strenuous endeavors that kept me in shape. During the summer I worked as a lifeguard at the Girl Scout camp or at Soldier Field when not traveling around playing in tennis tournaments. Swimming season ended in March after the state meet. I then had time to work after school for our neighbor Dr. Kendall, washing bottles and test tubes in his research lab at the Mayo Clinic. This experience prompted an interest in chemistry and the idea that it could become my vocation. I was eager to give it a try. After all, experimental medicine was an open field—and a theater for the development of all sorts of cures for human ailments.

Piano lessons took up much of my spare time from the ages of thirteen to seventeen. My teacher, Hazel Martin, had her studio in the Bethel Lutheran Church next to the library. She was a musical taskmaster for sure. With the yearly recital in mind, she assigned each of us a different piece and expected us to work on that one composition for the entire year. In theory this meant we could have it memorized and letter-perfect by performance time. At recitals people would remark about the amazing results she got from her students.

One year my assignment was Debussy's "Clare de Lune." I loved it and practiced diligently. Come recital time, I knew it well and hoped that everything was under control. Miss Martin was standing off-stage, behind a curtain. I played the introduction and the first page without a flaw—and that was when my memory left me. All I could do was repeat the beginning over and over while Miss Martin frantically tried to give *sotto voce* clues to the next movement. It was plain that while I could play the score flawlessly in private, the stress of performing in front of an audience was enough to rob me of my confidence.

One time Miss Martin decided I should learn to play the church pipe organ. The keyboards were no problem; it was the pedals that were my downfall. I was constantly checking to see where to put my feet. I don't remember which one of us gave up first. I tell people I stopped due to a bruised chin, because Miss Martin would tap me under the chin as a reminder to keep my head up. The piano was challenge enough and has remained an ongoing pleasure to this day.

In 1932 the Great Depression was in full swing. People didn't just talk about it; they lived it. Jobs were scarce to non-existent. There was no way it could be called a mere recession when all of the developed countries were suffering. At sixteen, I had just completed my junior year in high school. The Olympics were being held in Los Angeles that year, and athletes were coming from all over the world. At the same time twenty-five thousand World War I veterans were gathering in Washington, DC. In 1924 Congress had authorized a soldiers' bonus to be paid in 1945. Each veteran was to receive five hundred dollars, but the government hadn't come up with the funds yet. That rag-tag "bonus army" wanted it paid immediately. They had put together tin and cardboard shacks for shelter and vowed to stay until their pleas were heard and answered.

The situation was tense and could have led to serious trouble. General McArthur was anxious to clear them out and said he would do whatever it took. Slightly more than a decade later, he would be holding forth in an altogether different theater of action.

RIDING THE RAILS

Kids my age didn't pay much attention to what was happening in Washington, DC, however. We were much more interested in Los Angeles! I don't think my friend Fred Kissling and I entertained ideas of going there, but we did think it would be fun to hop a freight train to northern Minnesota and spend some of the summer swimming in the cool waters of those northern lakes. Fred and I were swimming rivals and had become good friends. He was from Winona but had come to Rochester for a short visit.

Late one afternoon we hitched a ride to Minneapolis to explore the Northern Pacific freight yards. We had heard that riding the rails was a cheap way to get from one place to another. Many men were doing it. They weren't hobos, just ordinary fellows trying to find jobs. We talked to one of them and he pointed to a couple of trains, saying that one would take us to Brainard, Minnesota, up in lake country. The other was heading west to California. We looked at each other with the same thought. Here was the means to travel— why dally any longer?

Years later Fred remembered that I was the one who suggested we get on the westbound train, promising that my Aunt Floss in Los Angeles would take us in!

He even remembered what we took with us: a loaf of bread, a jar of peanut butter, and a few cans of beans. Our only clothes were the ones we were wearing, and between us we had seven dollars in cash. I probably told that story of getting on the wrong train so many times that I came to believe it myself. At any rate, we crawled into an empty boxcar and made ourselves comfortable on a pile of straw while we waited for the three whistle toots signaling that the freight was on its way out of the yard. If we had any doubts about the wisdom of what we were doing, we didn't share them. Darkness had settled by the time the whistle finally tooted, and with a jerk and a rattle the cars began to move. We were on our way to an unscheduled adventure. It was too dark to see any landmarks that would give us clues about the route we were on. Soon the rhythmic clickety-clack of the wheels over the rail joints lulled us to sleep.

At dawn the train slowed down and we left our bed of straw to take a look. We were anxious to see how far we had traveled overnight. We spotted a sign telling us we had arrived in Fargo, North Dakota. Minnesota's ten thousand lakes were far behind us. We weren't concerned about how long our bread and beans and peanut butter would last. I knew my Aunt Floss would welcome a visit. Besides, the Olympics were on. That knowledge heightened our anticipation. Maybe we could see some of the events.

Our next stop was Deer Lodge, Montana. We were welcomed by a couple of local constables who rounded up the dozen or so "space-available" travelers and marched us into town. Needless to say, we had visions of winding up in the clink. We needn't have worried. Our destination turned out to be a soup kitchen, a.k.a. beanery, located in an old house across the street from the jail. The living room had been converted into a dining hall. Our table was a long counter covered with galvanized metal. The menu was beans and bread washed down with black coffee. We had been eating our own canned beans along the way, but these were hot and tasty, a welcome variation from Van de Camp's. When the last man had tucked away his grub, we were escorted single-file to the rail yards at the west end of the city. Here our escorts politely suggested that we take the first train out of town. We didn't have long to wait. In those years most freight was carried by rail, meaning that every day six to ten trains passed through Deer Lodge.

Another twenty-four hours on the rails brought us to Pasco, Washington. Since the train didn't have a dining car, and since our beans and bread were a fading memory, we decided to break up our trip and work awhile. It happened that the Pasco melon harvest was in full swing. The pay was twenty-five cents an hour, plus all the melons we could eat. They tasted wonderful and were cool and juicy, so it didn't take us long to discover that they could have been marketed as a substitute for Ex-Lax! We quickly found the well-worn path to the privy at one end of the huge field.

Two days later we climbed aboard a Southern Pacific boxcar headed towards Los Angeles. By then we were beginning to feel like seasoned travelers. We knew we weren't going to the land of milk and honey, but Southern California had other attractions. There was Hollywood and all those glamorous movie stars, plus of course the Olympics.

We weren't like Alice, falling down a rabbit hole. Our first view of Hollywood was from the back of an old truck roaring down San Fernando Boulevard. Coming into Glendale, we noticed all the airports that dotted the area, and the little wooden and canvas planes tethered alongside their runways. A bit further down the road, the driver dropped us at curbside and went on his way. With no map, we hadn't a clue how to find our way to the only person I knew, my Aunt Floss, who lived at 612 Laurel Avenue in Hollywood.

A short time later we had the good fortune to be picked up by a passing motorist with a map who was kind enough to take us to our destination. My favorite aunt greeted as if we were long-lost sons. The first thing on the agenda were much-needed baths. We spent the rest of the evening filling and refilling our empty stomachs and resting our tired bodies on the soft sofa and chairs—all the while talking nonstop about our unconventional cross-country trip. (No doubt Aunt Floss made a few discrete phone calls to our parents that evening.) Eventually we went to bed, a real honest-to-gosh bed, infinitely better than a pile of straw.

The next morning a friend from Rochester showed up to give us a tour of Pasadena. Riding down Orange Grove Avenue, we were practically goggle-eyed as Bob pointed out the palatial homes of millionaires such as William Wrigley and R.W. Gabriel. At six o'clock we headed down Atlantic Avenue to Balboa for a fabulous dinner and an evening at the summer home of one of Bob's female friends. Sitting on her veranda, we described our travels and listened to chitchat about local celebrities.

The next day we were slug-a-beds for sure, sleeping until mid-morning. After lunch we drove to Exposition Park near the Olympic Village. The Los Angeles Museum of History, Science, and Arts occupied a nine-acre complex that included a beautiful sunken garden. We spent most of the afternoon viewing the Olympic Art Exhibition and came away feeling that the artistry of Californians rivaled that of the Greeks.

That evening Aunt Floss took us to the famous Carthay Circle Theater to see John Boles in the movie *Backstreet*. The Carthay was one of the more exclusive movie houses in Los Angeles. It had a limited seating capacity and showed only the latest and best films. The sidewalls of the theater were filled with huge life-sized paintings of Western scenes. A carpeted stairway led to a mezzanine lounge decorated with more Western paintings. During intermission the ushers passed out paper cups filled with ice-cold spring water. The movie was accompanied by an outstanding orchestra and supported by a unique live stage show entitled "The Olympiad." We felt we were being royally entertained in the lap of luxury.

There was much to see and do, but after ten days of sightseeing, reality began to set in. With a jolt, we knew it was time to think about getting back home to Minnesota. School bells would soon be ringing! We didn't relish the idea of hopping freight trains for the return trip and decided that the Greyhound Bus service sounded pretty good. We needed money for tickets so I wired my parents. Right away Western Union called to say that a check was waiting for me. Fred and I raced down to their office to collect it. But when I opened the envelope, I felt as though my legs had been knocked out from under me.

It took a moment or two to get myself together. I felt a bit of anger and a lot of resentment—followed by dismay. The check was for ten dollars! What were we going to do now? I was sure that if it had been up to my mother she would have sent the entire amount, but I knew it wasn't just her decision. She and Pop had no doubt talked it over. There was a message in that ten-dollar check— it might as well have been printed across the face in bold type. "You got yourself out there; now get yourself home."

I could hear Pop saying those words, which would have been followed by Mom saying, "But Oscar, they have to eat." I learned later that Pop figured I would probably decide to stay another two weeks if I received the full bus fare.

Aunt Floss was sympathetic but she didn't undermine my parents by offering to pay our way home. The next morning she drove us the considerable distance to the eastern edge of Los Angeles. We found ourselves standing in the shade of a palm tree, hoping to ride our thumbs all the way to Mecca (Rochester).

We had experienced ten days of glitz, glamour, pseudo-Spanish haciendas, and palm trees—and now we wanted (needed) to get home, the sooner the better. We wouldn't starve along the way: our ten dollars would buy a lot of hamburgers. Prices those days ranged from five cents to a quarter. The coins in your pocket decided the size of your appetite.

Before long we saw some sort of vehicle coming toward us, its image distorted by the heat shimmering off the blacktop. It was a truck. We stuck up our thumbs, plastered smiles on our faces, and hoped it would pick us up. We weren't expecting a limousine, so anything with four wheels and a running motor would do. That truck didn't stop. Time passed but no other vehicle did. Since we had only five days until school started, we finally had to give up on the idea of hitchhiking. Our only other option was to ride the rails. Most of the eastbound freights slowed at Riverside. We found an empty boxcar and with considerable relief were soon on the way in our steel-wheeled stateroom.

We arrived in Sioux City, Iowa, on a Saturday afternoon and discovered that the first train north to Minnesota was a local passenger service. In the past we had ridden on the rears of cars by standing on the bumper and hanging onto the spare tire, so we figured that hanging onto a passenger coach wouldn't be much different. When it came along, we grabbed the handholds on the three-rung ladder that joined the cars as if we had been doing it for years. Forty miles north, the trained stopped in Rock Rapids. Unfortunately, a railroad bull spotted us.

The detective herded us into a corner at the depot and kept us there until the train was a couple of hundred yards down the track. Before letting us go, he advised us that what we were doing was extremely dangerous. (By that time we were out of money and felt that starvation was dangerous too.) He directed us to the local jail, where I called home and explained our predicament. Pop said he would send my brother Richard with the family car to pick us up.

Kissling and I slept in the jail that night. In the morning I spotted our Buick parked out in the street. Rich treated us to a big breakfast, and suddenly the world seemed much brighter. We were going to make it home in time to begin our senior year.

That was the same year I fell in love—with flying! My first airplane ride was with Fred Toogood, a family friend who sold sightseeing rides over Rochester. I'll never forget crawling into the cockpit of that fabric-and-wood crate, smelling the hot engine oil, and feeling the slipstream whipping my face when I poked my head over the side to watch the spectacular panorama unfolding below.

Toogood's plane was a World War I Curtis JN-4D bi-plane called a Jenny. The wings were covered with linen, stretched as tightly as possible and then coated with some kind of lacquer or "dope" that caused it to shrink as tight as a drumhead. Actually, it was a pretty durable surface. Bracing wires were stretched diagonally between the wing and struts to form an X. I heard that piano wire was often used. The plane had few instruments, so you had to fly by feel. The wind whistled through the wires, making a sound that got louder and more high-pitched as the speed increased. When you could hear it, you knew you were going too fast to attempt a landing. At slow speeds the low-pitched tone of the wires barely whispered, a sign that you were approaching a stall condition.

With only a fragile wooden frame and a layer of fabric between me and my avian environment, I got the feel of it much as I imagine birds do when they fly—reading the wind second by second and using their wings and tails to maneuver themselves. For me that first flight was far from a fearsome experience; I was hooked and wanted to learn how to fly one of those man-made birds.

I memorized the takeoff procedure as if my life depended upon it. Toogood answered my questions about the plane itself. From him I learned that its laminated wood prop, driven by a 90-horsepower Curtis OX-5 motor, gave it a maximum level speed of 75 miles per hour, that its wingspan was 43 feet, and that it weighed about 2,100 pounds. The OX-5 had no electric starter, so starting it called for a special liturgy. First the mechanic yelled "OFF." Then the pilot put the ignition switch in the *off* position and hollered "OFF" back. Next the mechanic rotated the prop a couple of turns to prime the engine and yelled "ON" in his loudest voice. When the prop blades were in the near-vertical position, he reached up while standing on tiptoe and grasped the tip of the blade with both hands. With a swift thrust and a kick of his leg, he swung the prop blade in a downward arc and hoped the engine would fire.

During World War I the Jenny was the standard trainer for the Signal Corps. More than six thousand of them were built. After the war many were deemed surplus by the military, and civilians bought them to "barnstorm" around the country. It was in that way that civilians had their first look at an airplane, marveled at the acrobatics the pilots could take them through, and then parted with hard-earned cash to take a ride aloft. The Jenny was chosen to deliver the first airmail between Washington, Philadelphia, and New York City. Unfortunately, the pilot headed in the wrong direction and landed in Maryland instead of Philadelphia. Eventually the mail was put on a northbound train, leaving the Signal Corps feeling more than a little humiliated.

Little did I realize that a decade later I would be sitting behind the controls of a Lockheed P-38, pushing the throttles of two liquid-cooled, super-charged Allison engines rated at 1,200 horsepower each and hurtling through the air at more than 400 miles per hour.

My interest in flying turned out to be more than a teenage crush. In 1933, while attending junior college, I took a series of flying lessons. My first solo flight was in a tiny Aeronca C-3, a high-wing monoplane powered by a four-cylinder Continental motor rated at forty horsepower. Simple heel-actuated brakes and a fixed tailskid made taxiing in a crosswind especially tricky. The rental charge for solo time in those days was seven dollars an hour. I earned it by mopping the white tile floors in my father's drugstore every morning before school.

That summer I got a job that paid thirty-two cents an hour at the Reid Murdock corn-canning factory on the south edge of the city. I worked with the crew in a boxcar, loading cans into a chute that carried them to the filling machine inside the factory. It was fast work. If we wanted to rest, we would turn a few cans upside down. When they came to the filling machine, the corn would spill out onto the floor. Red lights would flash, alarm bells would ring, and the line would shut down while a crew cleaned up the mess. The empties came from three different boxcars so the foreman could never tell who was the culprit.

That year I also hoped to firm up my plans for the future. I intended to major in chemistry but my interest in sports was still alive. The junior college didn't have a swimming team so I tried out for football. I ended up on the bench, waiting for one of the backfield to get hurt.

The next year I enrolled at the University of Minnesota to pursue chemical engineering, but it didn't take long to find out that I lacked the patience to sit on a stool in the lab all afternoon waiting for precipitates to filter through. I decided to change course and auditioned in the music department, thinking that I would enjoy teaching music in a public school. My playing did not impress the panel. They said that music would make a nice avocation for me, but not a profession. That put a damper on my spirits. I decided the university was too big for me and returned home that spring to work at Pop's drugstore. I still had time to get in some tennis during the summer.

In 1935 my brother Walt was the head football coach at Sioux Falls College, a Baptist school. In those days they did not use a kicking tee. One of the players had to hold the ball for the kick-off. With only twenty-one players, there was no one to hold the ball during scrimmages between the first and second teams. Walt said I could be a reserve on the team if I wasn't planning to go away to college that year. At least I could hold the ball for practice kick-offs. I accepted his offer and moved to Sioux Falls. Learning the plays for each of the backfield positions was good practice, but actual scrimmages were exhausting. A missed blocking assignment was rewarded with extra laps around the track at the end of the day. I didn't mind being a benchwarmer during a game, but dreaded the times when someone got hurt and a substitute was needed.

The next year I wasn't sure what to do. I had been in and out of three different schools. I imagine that by then my parents were a little disturbed by my indecisiveness. Ham radio appealed to me early on and became my hobby. I spent many happy hours contacting other operators and tinkering with the radio itself.

Perhaps electrical engineering would be the slot for me. Iowa State College at Ames was one of the top engineering schools in the country and had the advantage of being close to home. Only a few of my credits from the three other schools were accepted, however, so for the fourth time I enrolled in a new school as a freshman.

Tuition and books cost about two hundred dollars a year. I rented a room in a private home for ten dollars a week. My commercial radio operator's license landed me a part-time job as an engineer at the college broadcast station, WOI. The fifty-cents-an-hour wage was double what I was making as a soda jerk in a drugstore across the street from the college.

Earning spots on the varsity tennis and swimming teams gave me a respite from academia. My specialty swimming events were the 220- and 440-yard races. I was awarded a varsity letter each year but didn't break any records. The coach said I had a great stroke but just swam in the same spot too long.

Even though fraternity life beckoned, I felt I had neither the time nor the money to get involved. I had to maintain my focus this time or my college days would surely be over. But Don Allen, a swim teammate, invited me for Monday night supper at the Phi Delta Theta house so many times that I finally felt obligated to affiliate. In the fall of 1939 I was initiated and became a Brother in Bond.

I matured a lot in those early indecisive years. In 1940, after graduating from Iowa State College with a B.S. degree in electrical engineering, I landed a job working for Major Edwin H. Armstrong. Now known as the "father of FM," he was working on an experimental FM radio at his station in Alpine, New Jersey. At this stage we spent a lot of time testing antennae. The broadcast frequencies we used were primarily limited to line-of-sight distances, so antenna height was a major factor in determining the distances at which FM signals could be heard.

The radio tower at Alpine was four hundred feet high and of a unique design. Two horizontal wings stretched out from the vertical structure that supported the various types of high-frequency antennae. A steel stairs led from the ground to the platform on which the antennae and test equipment were mounted. It was quite a job to get ourselves—let alone various parts and tools—up there. To save time and effort, we took our lunch and spent the whole day four hundred feet in the air.

At the top of the tower was a warning beacon. One of my jobs was to replace the light at regular intervals. That precaution reduced the possibility of failure, which could put night-flying pilots in mortal danger. It was scary work. Sometimes the wind whistled around me at a pretty good clip. I yearned for the security of solid ground but was compensated with a gorgeous view of New York City twenty miles to the south. My initial assignment was to work the night shift on the broadcast transmitter. In that role I served as engineer, announcer, and program director. It was the privilege of the duty engineer to select the recordings for that evening's program. We had a wonderful library of high-fidelity classical music, so I was as happy as a kid in a candy store.

Working nights gave me lots of free time during the day. I didn't have a car, but I did have a lightweight touring bicycle. From time to time I escaped the work ethic by loading my bike onto a train at Tenafly for a trip up the Hudson River to West Point. The military academy sat on a bluff above the river, its ramparts beautiful in a rugged sort of way. The return trip to Alpine was an easy downhill ride. From that ground-level perspective the scenery was exhilarating and wonderful. I always got back in plenty of time for my night shift as disc jockey cum engineer.

INTO THE WILD BLUE YONDER

Around this time I was about to start a new chapter in my life, one that I could not have imagined. Rumblings of war in Europe were beginning to be heard, along with the possibility that the United States could be drawn into it. In preparation for that eventuality, Congress enacted the Selective Service bill. I decided to join up without waiting for my number to be called. Word was out that by getting in early, volunteers would have a better chance of receiving the assignments they wanted. In previous years I had chosen paths that led to indecision and a certain amount of frustration. Now I was choosing one that would lead in an unexpected direction and dramatically influence the rest of my life.

On February 27, 1941 I received a postcard from the local Selective Service Board at Bergenfield, New Jersey, saying I was classified 1-A and scheduled for induction on March 17. Having spent several years as a ham radio operator, and also being the proud holder of a degree in electrical engineering, I assumed I would wind up in the Signal Corps. However, I was overlooking the military's logic of placing square pegs in round holes. I wound up in tent city at Fort Dix, New Jersey. A few weeks later I was on a troop train bound for Fort Knox, Kentucky, to join the First Armored Forces. My first assignment was KP duty. I sat on the veranda behind the mess hall and flattened empty Carnation condensed milk cans with a hatchet so they wouldn't take up so much room in the garbage pit. That duty didn't add anything positive to my impression of playing soldier.

The following week I finally had the opportunity to be a real soldier serving his country. Armed with a wooden baton and a flashlight, I went out into the night to patrol the motor pool, counting the vehicles every other circuit and reporting the results to the corporal of the guard. I had no idea what would happen should I come up with the wrong count—and I never got a chance to find out.

A (TDY) temporary duty assignment to Godman Field in Louisville during an air show put on by pilots from Selfridge Field, Michigan, re-awakened my love of flying. I knew then that there was no way I would be happy as a tank driver. Since I hadn't heard from the Signal Corps, I applied for aviation cadet training and got sent to Parks Air College in Sikeston, Missouri. There I was introduced to my all-time favorite plane—the Stearman, a bi-plane with a 250-horsepower radial engine and an open cockpit.

20

The rush of the slipstream and the smell of hot engine oil reminded me of my first ride in that old WWI Curtis Jenny. Again I was filled with the excitement and joy I had felt as a sixteen-year-old, and was most anxious to get on with the business of flying. Cadet life was wonderful: we had plenty of good food, interesting ground-school classes, good flying weather, and an increase in pay. (As cadets we got seventy-five dollars per month, more than twice the thirty dollars that privates made.)

For a while I wondered if I would ever get to fly solo. Most of my classmates had soloed after only seven or eight hours of dual instruction—and my logbook registered eleven hours! That old specter, washout, hovered over my shoulder. Then late one afternoon my instructor took me for a ride. We landed at one of our remote satellite training fields. Parking the plane alongside the fence, we sat and talked for a while with the engine still running. Suddenly he climbed out and said, "OK, Mr. Fred, it's time to go it alone."

I doubt that my voice quavered, but I did ask, "Why are you doing this to me? I don't think I'm quite ready." With a grin he replied, "I think you are. During these past few weeks I've seen you make every mistake in the book and I've shown you how to recover. Actually, I'll be more comfortable watching you solo than I was with some of those hotshots who did it after only six or seven hours of dual."

As I taxied upwind to the takeoff position, I noticed that the rudder pedals had a completely different feel. Only then did I fully realize that I was indeed on my own. This time there would be no safety net, no instructor at my side telling me how to correct a mistake. My heart had been beating a regular tattoo against my ribs, but those extra hours of study and practice, along with the fact that my instructor had confidence in me, steadied my nerves and gave me confidence in myself. I took the bird up like a pro. Joy, oh joy! I was flying on my own. My grin was so wide that if there had been bugs up there, they would have been plastered all over my teeth.

When I landed, the instructor congratulated me and gave me some sage advice. "If you ever make a flight in which you don't learn at least one new thing, it will be time to hang up your goggles."

Our next post was Randolph Field for basic training in a BT-9, a low-wing monoplane with a fixed landing gear and a variable-pitch prop. We were introduced to night flying, and it wasn't at all unusual to arrive at the flight line in the morning and see an aircraft on its nose in the middle of the field. Some cadet had hit the brakes too hard, too early.

On December 7, 1941, the news from Pearl Harbor brought a change in the tempo of activity at Randolph. Instructors were ticked off because all leaves were canceled and cadets were restricted to base. Rumors abounded. One report had it that a Japanese carrier had entered the Gulf of California. I never learned whether or not there was any truth to it. What happened at Pearl Harbor made it very plain that we weren't playing a game: this was deadly serious business. A few days later we got word that our class of 42-C would graduate two weeks early.

After graduation our class was split in two. Half were sent to Brownsville, Texas, while the rest of us went across town to Brooks Field for advanced training. There we were introduced to the AT-6, a more complex aircraft. Its landing gear could be raised to reduce drag and then lowered for landing. Remembering that all-important step kept us on our toes. More than one cadet made an extra turn around the field before it became an automatic move. This plane had a narrow "tread" as it were, giving it built-in ground-loop characteristics.

An important moment in our cadet life was the day we got fitted for uniforms at the tailor shop in San Antonio. Who could ever forget those elegant "pink" cords that are collector's items today? We had been classified as airmen, but now we had the look of airmen as well—and our pride was visible in the set of every pair of shoulders.

After receiving our gold second-lieutenant bars, some of our class members were posted to Kelly Field in San Antonio for fighter training. Others went to Georgia for bomber school, while a few of the "elite," who were later to become part of the 8th Photo Squadron, remained at Brooks to fly the O-52's. These planes had originally been built for the navy, but they were underpowered for carrier duty and so given to the Army Air Cadet Corps to be used as trainers. We spent several weeks chauffeuring newly commissioned second lieutenants from West Point. They took aerial pictures and sighted targets for artillery exercises from the back seats of our O-52's, a feat that should have earned them medals for bravery!

A selector valve and a hand-operated pump supplied the hydraulic pressure for the flaps and wheels on the O-52. After getting airborne, we had to retract the wheels quickly in order to reduce drag. Immediately thereafter it was standard operating procedure (SOP) to turn the selector valve and slowly pump up the flaps. I remember one occasion in which the pilot pumped up the flaps before retracting the wheels. The squadron mess hall stood just a few yards off the end of the runway. As the flaps pulled up, the aircraft gradually lost altitude and gently mushed through the roof of the mess hall. Fortunately the room was empty, so the only "casualties" were a red-faced second lieutenant pilot and the frightened observer in the rear seat. I expect they were a bit wobbly-legged by the time they were extricated from that mess.

When we had done our bit at Brooks Field, we went by rail to Riverside, California to join Lieutenant Colonel Frank Dunn and the "B" flight of the 8th Photo Squadron. The "A" flight had already departed for Australia en route to New Guinea. By this time we had been transferred so often that getting settled and learning our way around was just a routine exercise.

In Riverside we were introduced to the F-4, a photo version of the Lockheed P-38 Lightning. Transitioning from the O-52 to the twin-engine P-38 was an all-or-nothing experience, since none of the planes was outfitted for dual instruction. The twin-engine Curtis, which was supposed to give us single-engine pilots some multi-engine experience, was more difficult to fly than the P-38. Colonel Dunn told us we could fly the Curtis trainer *after* we checked out in the Lightning.

The P-38 was originally designed to be a high-speed, long-range fighter aircraft. Its two turbo-charged, liquid-cooled engines gave it a top speed of over 400 miles per hour at a service ceiling of 40,000 feet, and a maximum range of almost 2,300 miles. These capabilities made it ideal for use as a photo-reconnaissance aircraft. Since we would be alone on our missions, we had to not only be the pilot, but also the navigator, the radio operator, and the cameraman.

We used a retractable ladder on the rear of the fuselage to access the cockpit. After we made it onto the wing, we literally had to crawl under the V-shaped high-frequency antenna that stretched from the cockpit canopy to the two tail sections. The pilot's manual omitted any instructions on how to abandon the aircraft in case of emergency. Evidently they thought that with enough positive thinking, an emergency would never arise. More about that later!

After squeezing into the pilot's seat, we were required to go through a twenty-two-point checklist. At first glance the instrument panel was mind-boggling—a nightmare of eighteen different control knobs and switches, plus twenty-five gauges and indicator instruments.

Added to all this was tricycle landing gear. My first taxi run should have been an adventure, but it nearly ended in disaster. I did a quick 180-degree turn and dusted off the CO (commanding officer) with my backwash—sort of like a kid doing a wheelie with his hot-rod. It was probably a good thing I couldn't hear what he said. But after some more ground taxi runs and a few hours of studying the instruction manual, it would be time to take the ship up into the WILD BLUE YONDER.

Came the day and the time! I taxied down to the south end of the 10,000-foot runway and went through the engine run-up, checking the propeller controls and mags. The tower cleared me for takeoff. I lined up on the runway, stomped on the toe brakes, and opened the throttles to 40 inches of manifold pressure. By the time the rpm's reached 3,000, the turbines were screaming. I released the brakes and the aircraft leaped forward. I was airborne by the time I passed the 2,000-feet runway marker. Easing back on the control column, I put the ship into a gentle climb to an altitude of 1,500 feet. Then, glancing down at the instrument panel, I was shocked to find the airspeed needle at zero as I climbed at a rate of nearly 1,000 feet per second—my first experience with levitation. According to my cheering fans on the flight line, I told the control tower that I had no air speed and requested permission to make an emergency landing.

When I got lined up on the runway, I spotted a fire truck and an ambulance—which did nothing to assure me that my first solo landing in a P-38 was going to be picture-perfect. I have no idea at what speed I touched down. Lots of blue smoke shot out behind the tires, and folks watching said it was the hottest landing they had ever seen at March Field. Apparently I had plenty of airspeed, but the protective cover, with its red warning flag, was still attached to the pito tube—which of course made the airspeed gauge inoperative.

The words of my primary instructor were prophetic. "Fred, if you don't learn something new on every flight, it's time to hang up your goggles." I had scared myself for sure, but never recalled radioing for permission to land. This time I learned that a "walk-around" was an essential part of every pre-flight inspection. That was something I never again forgot.

With about five hours of solo time under my belt, my CO assigned me the task of ferrying one of the planes to the Lockheed Mod-Center at Dallas for camera equipment installation. Apparently it was more cost-effective to take a standard production fighter with all its armament to another facility for the camera modification.

This two-thousand-mile cross-country training exercise gave me another chance to learn something new. By the time I got to El Paso the gas gauges were dipping down near the one-fourth level, so I decided to drop into Biggs Field and top off the tanks before the long ride across the Texas plains. Not only did this allow me to stretch my legs, but walking into the operations office, signing a chit for 250 gallons of 100-octane gas, and casually climbing back into my P-38 (yes, by then I was actually beginning to feel possessive about it) also gave me a sense of power.

My recent lesson prompted me to carefully go through every step of pre-flight routine. Fortunately, the approaches to Biggs Field stretch out for several miles over flat terrain. The tower cleared me for take-off and moments later I was airborne. Suddenly the rpm's on the starboard engine went past the red line and the aircraft began to yaw. Almost immediately I realized that the prop had gone into flat pitch (a not-uncommon problem with Curtis Electric props). Once again I had to abort the flight. After feathering the prop and shutting off the engine, I had the exciting experience of making my first single-engine landing. I gave myself a mental pat on the back for handling the problem "according to the book."

By the time I landed at Love Field in Dallas, I considered myself a fully certified P-38 pilot. My log book showed a total of ten hours—yes, ten hours of flying that temperamental bird, most of it within sight of March Field.

Back in March Field a week later, rumors began to circulate that we would soon be getting orders to ship overseas. We had expected to face that possibility, and knew that the many weeks of study, instruction, and flight time were preparing us for it, but our excitement was mixed with a bit of fear as well—not much different from when we were kids flying down those snowy hills on our Flexible Flyers.

Before the actual orders arrived, however, we got to enjoy a delightful interlude. I had become quite popular when my squadron-mates learned of my Hollywood connection. My Aunt Floss was secretary to Winifred Sheehan, one of the vice presidents of Twentieth Century Fox and an entree to some of the young starlets who were eager to contribute to the war effort. That's how it happened that Lieutenants Post, Guerry, and Hargesheimer got to spend an evening dancing at the Palladium with three lovely young ladies named Barbara Britton, Linda Darnell, and Donna Reed. We felt we were pretty handsome fellows in our uniforms, and a credit to the military as well. The fact that publicity pictures were taken did nothing to damage our egos.

Next on our schedule was a train ride to Oakland. General orders had put us on alert to be ready to sail at any moment. Since we had one last day of shore leave to explore the sights of San Francisco, we went to the Top of the Mark (*the* popular choice for a night on the town in those days). Only the presence of numerous uniformed young men hinted that a war was in progress.

PHOTO MISSION NUMBER FORTY-NINE

On the morning of June 15, 1942, we hoisted our duffle bags over our shoulders and marched down to the wharf. Waiting for us was a flagship of the Matson Line, the *Matsonia*. In peacetime she could accommodate fifteen hundred passengers. Now five thousand khaki-clad GIs were herded on board for an "all-expense-paid cruise" to the South Pacific.

It was after dark when two tugboats came alongside, edged us away from the dock, and towed us out into the harbor. A few minutes later we were gliding under the Golden Gate Bridge. For the next twenty-six days we zigzagged across the Pacific towards Australia at a speed of eighteen knots. Lookouts anxiously kept watch for enemy submarines, hoping against hope that the Japanese wouldn't spot us. On the fourth day we joined three other ships to form a convoy. Rumor had it that one of them was crewed by Russian women. Each time we zagged, all five thousand of us scrambled to the opposite side of the ship in search of a better view. It was plain that although we had left family and friends behind, our libidos were still very much with us!

The *Matsonia* had been chartered by the U.S. Army Transport Services. The contract stipulated that the officers be fed in the main dining room. This arrangement turned out to be an embarrassment for the pilots in our squadron. While we were enjoying gourmet selections from printed menus, the enlisted personnel were eating canned chicken twice a day. After a few days they would have appreciated anything that didn't cluck or crow.

The USN *Indianapolis* joined our convoy at Auckland, New Zealand, and shepherded us to Australia through water that was crawling with enemy submarines. Finally, twenty-eight days after leaving San Francisco, we arrived in Melbourne. A brass band and a bevy of beautiful girls gave us a warm welcome.

After a couple of weeks billeted in the Melbourne Cricket Grounds, a stadium that seats 100,000 people, we boarded a train for Townsville about two thousand miles to the north. Details of that journey would fill a book by itself. For five days we rode in the economy section, which had no diner and no sleeping accommodations. At about four every afternoon, we stopped out in the middle of nowhere while the crew got out their billy tins and had "a cuppa and bickies." Bickies is short for biscuits—not our kind of biscuits, but a sort of cookie that to our taste isn't very sweet. At mealtimes we stopped at some primitive depot and dined on the usual fare—Ausie sausages, hard rolls, and chicory coffee. I began to wonder if the people in that part of the world knew what a cup of "real" coffee tasted like.

When we reached Albany on the border between Victoria and New South Wales, there was a change in rail gauge, which meant a change in trains. All of our equipment, including heavy spare aircraft engines, had to be transferred onto another flatcar. This task was repeated a few days later when we crossed from New South Wales into Queensland. Lavatory facilities were minimal, which meant there was always a line at the loo. We had to use our metal helmets for basins when we wanted to shave.

Finally we reached Garbutt Field to join up with the "A" flight of the 8th Photo Reconnaissance Squadron under the command of Colonel Karl Polifka. During our stay we had a chance to log a few more hours in the F-4. We also had a side trip to Darwin to take some photo strips for a mapping project. It was Lieutenant George Newton's first mission as a command pilot on the B-17. I joined the crew as navigator and proceeded to guide us to a landing at the wrong airstrip.

Only a few visual checkpoints are found across the northern territory of Australia. With the mission station at Roper River behind us, we saw nothing but hundreds of miles of barren land. When an airstrip appeared on the horizon, I was certain it was our destination. We touched down on the dirt runway and Newton commented that it seemed much shorter than the charts indicated. We didn't discover we were in the wrong place until we were drinking a cold squash with the RAAF folks based at this unnamed airfield.

It was the first time an airplane as big as our B-17 had ever landed there. Bachelor Field, our intended destination, was just thirty kilometers down the road, but we were faced with the problem of getting our bird airborne again. Sweat gleamed on every inch of Newton's exposed skin as we roared down that short runway and the co-pilot called out the air speed. When we cleared the gum trees with barely a foot to spare, the crew heaved a collective sigh of relief.

Until the airstrip at Schwimmer airdrome, about fourteen miles from Port Moresby, was completed, Townsville was to be our home base. During those six weeks we flew our photo missions from the main field at Port Moresby.

August 13, 1942, was a sad day for the 8th Photo. Lieutenant Paul Staller left Townsville and headed for Port Moresby via Horne Island on the northeastern tip of Australia. He reached the island safely, but waited until nearly sundown to continue on to Moresby. He did not arrive there, however, and a check of all the New Guinea airdromes failed to find any word of him. We assumed that his engines or navigation instruments had failed. Losing a man of Paul's caliber was a serious blow to the squadron. He was admired and loved by all of us, and his disappearance brought home the fact that we were involved in an extremely serious enterprise. War was not a game: this could happen to any of us at any time.

The very fact that we were a young squadron, too young to be afraid of the unknown, helped us through that experience. Soon the excitement of what we were being trained to do overrode our misgivings. Each new mission was covered with a veneer of adventure. Taking off from Garbutt Field and heading out across the Coral Sea to Port Moresby, eight hundred miles to the north, with only a simple magnetic compass to guide us, was quite different from flying across dry land from California to Texas.

After Townsville, our home for the next several months was Fourteen-Mile airdrome at Port Moresby. We called it Laloki in honor of the river that flowed across the northwest end of the airstrip. The runway was laid down with pierced steel planking, a technology that made it possible to complete an airstrip in only a few days. An engineering battalion of black soldiers who really knew what they were doing built ours in record time.

Our living quarters were a series of pyramidal tents sprinkled among the scrub trees half a mile from the airdrome. My tent-mate was Alex Guerry, a good friend and skilled pilot from Sewanee, Tennessee who snacked on vitamin pills sent by his mother. We hadn't been there long before some of the local residents came around seeking work. One Australian shilling would get your laundry done if you furnished the soap. It didn't matter how large the load—one shirt or five shirts, the price was the same—so two or three of us would combine our clothes. A coconut also cost one shilling and was a welcome addition to GI fare.

The food wasn't too bad, considering the conditions. "SOS" (chipped beef on toast) was on the menu several times a week. And occasionally the "dynamite brigade" would supply the cooks with fresh fish by tossing a stick of dynamite into the water. The explosion would stun enough fish to feed the whole squadron.

One of our priority missions was taking pictures for maps. (Very few useful maps existed during the early part of the New Guinea campaign. The German admiralty charts showed only the coastlines and a few miles inland.) Our trimetrogon system of aerial photography used three cameras. One pointed straight down, while the others were offset at sixty-degree angles. At an altitude of twenty thousand feet, we could take a strip of pictures covering an area about forty miles wide. An electronic intervalometer clicked off the pictures at a rate determined by the altitude and speed of the plane. The pilot had to maintain a near-constant altitude, preferably within plus or minus fifty feet.

The New Guinea climate is not very favorable for aerial photography. Each morning we had a window of about an hour. Before nine the light was insufficient, and after ten the sky was often covered by a layer of cumulus clouds.

Staff Sergeant Glen Bowers was in charge of survival equipment, including our very important parachutes. It wasn't just a matter of packing them in their canvas cases. Because of the high humidity, it was necessary to inspect and often dry out the nylon. A damp chute could grow mold at a surprising rate. If we had to bail out, our lives depended on those chutes. (Practice jumps would have been a good idea, but for some reason no one was interested in doing them.) Glen's meticulous attention to every detail impressed me.

During the summer of 1942, the seizure of Port Moresby remained a priority of the Japanese forces. In May an attempted amphibious invasion had been thwarted in the battle of the Coral Sea. On July 21, enemy ground troops made a successful landing at Buna on the north coast of Papua New Guinea. By the end of August they had fought their way overland on the Kokoda Trail to within thirty miles of Port Moresby.

The following dates, extracted from Ole Olson's notes in the 8th Photo Squadron operations log, reveal the deeds and misdeeds of the men of that squadron.

Thursday, Sept 10, 1942

We expected to get started on our high-priority mapping project today, but Air Force decided that we should perform photo-reconnaissance of Northeast Papua. Following that plan, Hargesheimer took off at 0600 for a survey glance of the Buna area. He was followed at two-hour intervals by Major Polifka, Lt. Savage, Lt. Gardner, Lt. Rennels, and Major Polifka again. These were mainly orientation flights for the new pilots and nothing unusual happened in the air, but Lt. Gardner sadly but firmly bashed in the leading edge of 2139's right wing. The hard standings are set back in the trees and there isn't much room to swing the aircraft around.

Monday, September 14, 1942

Tragedy is certainly dogging our boys. Lt. Peterson departed at 0600 in 2098 for dawn patrol of northeast New Guinea, and nothing more was heard from him. After checking the airdromes, Major Polifka took off in search of him, but a general overcast at 5,000 feet made observation impossible. Pete is a swell person, one of the regular guys, and he will be sorely missed. These first missions are exceedingly difficult. The weather is always bad, and with no experience over the terrain, navigation is mostly by guess and by God. Best of luck Pete, we shall pray that you walk out.

Monday, September 21, 1942

Lt. Hargesheimer departed in ship 2177 this morning at 0919 hours. His mission was to photograph the Japanese airdrome at Lae in the Huon Gulf. He completed the mission, filming Lae, Salamaua, Buna and vicinity, and the Sanananda-Wairopi track. He returned to Laloki but the air raid warning at 1200 hours sent him out to sea, so he didn't get back to the drome until 1335 hours.

Wednesday, September 30, 1942

I don't know how you fellows are faring up there in the main camp, but I'd like to point out the hazardous manner in which we live down here on the flight line. Every night after we climb into our damp and clammy sacks, the wallabies pay the nearby grass a visit. Now that in itself may be just a normal habit of these little creatures, but with the Japanese just over the hill, the rustling of the grass and the odd thumping of the tail become a whole patrol of Japanese moving in on our little tent compound. The result is a bunch of trigger-happy fellows.

Well, last night, about an hour after turning in, we suddenly heard something crashing through the bush. Up jumped our automatic-weapons man, Roerig. With gun cocked and flashlight in hand, he cried out in a tremulous voice, "Who's there, who's there?" There was no answer. Once again, "Who's there, who-who-who's th-th-there?" Again no answer. After a moment of silence, there was a tremendous noise that would have passed as a Bronx cheer in other circumstances but turned out to be GI Thomas, who had finally found the straddle trench in the dark.

Sunday, November 1, 1942
Hargesheimer took the dawn flight to Lae this morning and on the way had a passel of trouble. The report obtained from him while he was still very excited is somewhat confusing, but the following approximates the truth. Hargy was skillfully flying on instruments when suddenly one supercharger cut out and at the same time the other engine ran away. This placed the excited one on his back. After losing 7,000 feet he managed to right his aircraft, and since the weather was bad he returned to base.

Friday, November 20, 1942
Joy reigned in the camp at suppertime when $2,300 in back pay was distributed among the men. The Sydney drain has been so great that hardly a farthing remained in camp. The great influx of folding money was used to pay off back debts and store up a reserve for future R&R trips to Australia. Corporal Jones of the cook shack received his usual treatment from the Finance Department. He has yet to be paid for his first day in the army.

The successful day was brought to a close by a movie under the hazy light of a beautiful tropical moon. *Too Many Girls* was the title of the picture, and though it was most entertaining, it did remind the fellows that there are too DAMN FEW girls around these parts.

Monday, February 22, 1943
The folks back in the States think this is Washington's Birthday, but all of us at Laloki think it should be changed to Slit Trench Day, for today revealed an epochal evolution of the human mind.

Many moons ago the 8th Photo moved from one side of the river to the other. Even then we were old and hard-bitten New Guineaites. Much time in slit trenches and the sound of air-raid sirens had bred contempt for the Japanese raids, so upon reaching our new home, only a few hardy souls started digging trenches. They soon laid aside their spades, lamenting that the ground was too hard and rocky to bother with. The general philosophy was that you could go to the top of the hill and the bombs wouldn't have much chance of hitting you anyway.

Now last night the Japanese chose Laloki as the target of opportunity and opened their bomb bays at the ungodly hour of 2 A.M. Ten bombs were dropped in a string from the runway to the Ninth Fighter camp, a mere hundred yards from our camp. Came the dawn, and on every side were 8th Photo men diligently throwing rock and clay with reckless abandon. Tonight finds the area a veritable maze of trenches, and now and then an occasional yell rends the air as another unwary fellow lands with a thud in the mud and water that soon showed up in the bottom of those trenches. As to the raid itself, for some reason nobody reached the haven of safety at the top of the hill. Hargesheimer and Sowers found cover under Fairbanks's jeep, and Guerry, always thinking of his better half, went under the jeep feet-first and left his head sticking out. I wish I had a picture of the three of them taking a shower by the listerbag when the bombs began to fall. Then there was Olson, who hit the dirt beside his bed with the sheet still wrapped around him. Post, the great mechanical genius, just stayed in his sack and kept asking what S.O.B. was driving a freight train past his bed.

The bombs straddled the runway, just missing on each side. Two bombs landed in the gasoline dump but hit only the piles of empties and threw dirt on the drums. Just to prove even a flood had its better points, the planes that might have been damaged were the ones evacuated to 12-Mile. Damage: nil. Casualties: oil on Guerry's cheeks.

Tuesday, June 1, 1943

Our energetic mess officer, Will Southard, his mind ever on his duties even while flying, landed at 30-Mile today and talked turkey with the natives for some fresh fruit. POG ["Pissed-Off Gardner"] covered the waterfront and even ventured into the mountains today. Two Bulldog-Wau strips and a series of K-18 shots on the trip, plus a few other items, left him completely devoid of film so he had to come home.

Hargesheimer carried on magnificently today. Off at 0800, he crossed the ranges and landed at Dobodura for more gas. There they pawned some dirty gas off on him. Upon taking off, his right engine produced so little power that he nearly took the control tower with him. He returned to Schwimmer and the trouble cleared up en route. He landed and took off again at 1000. He proceeded to Rabaul and got the pictures that were wanted. Such determination is worthy of commendation. Loos flew from Lae to Wewak and vicinity with good results.

Thursday, June 3, 1943
FLASH! Wire received this afternoon informing Captains Savage and Thomas to report to Pilot Replacement Depot, APO 923. You know what that means—the lucky bastards are on their way home. The place erupted in turmoil—much laughter and profanity, but Olson is over in the corner cursing his fate.

Air Task Force needed some photo ships for a special assignment. The two other flight leaders in our squadron were on temporary duty in Australia, so the squadron CO told me to pack my mosquito net and get "C" flight ready to move. At noon I climbed into *Eager Beaver* and pointed her nose up north across the twelve-thousand-foot peaks of the Owen Stanley Mountains, which divide central Papua. An hour later the wheels touched down on the steel matting of a new airstrip at Dobodura on the north coast. A jeep carrying a checkered flag came bouncing across the runway to guide me to a parking revetment, my home for the next few weeks.

At the operations hut a group of officers stood beside a map of New Britain discussing the next day's missions. It seemed that the Japanese were running supplies by barge from Rabaul along the north coast to reinforce their troops at Cape Gloucester. It was important to shut off this supply line because American forces were scheduled to make a landing there before the end of the year. Our task was to patrol up and down the north coast of New Britain, investigate any suspicious activities, and report any sightings by radio to our "medium" bombers on standby alert. We all felt this would be a welcome change from our routine photo-reconnaissance activities.

I went out on the sweep the first day but failed to see anything. Bad weather forced the pilot on the next day's trip to return to base early.

Obviously we were both disappointed not to find any targets for the B-25's. Two days later the weather cleared and I was determined to stir up some trouble. Shortly before lunch I left Dobodura in *Eager Beaver* and headed out across the Bismarck Sea toward the Vitiaz Straits that separate Finschhafen Peninsula from New Britain. The weather was threatening all the way, but *Eager Beaver* just pushed her nose right through the stuff.

When the dim outline of the south coast of New Britain broke through the haze, I contacted home base and tapped a position and weather report in Morse code. After much cluttering of the air with dots and dashes, I realized the signals officer had given me the wrong code-sequence sheet for that particular day. The radio report probably went into the wastebasket. *Eager Beaver* was impatient to move on so I sent a brief "nuts to you" and turned off the transmitter.

I could just barely see splotches of the coastline through breaks in the clouds and decided to drop down to the "deck" and have a better look. From there I could see surf breaking on the beach, and further along I spotted an outrigger canoe rocking on the waves. Two natives stopped paddling for a moment and waved a greeting. I let *Eager Beaver* dip her wings in salute. It was good to see human activity.

In a few minutes Rook Island appeared on the port side. Two passes around the island at low altitude revealed nothing, so I turned eastward across the channel to Cape Gloucester. The airdrome there was a deserted grass strip stretching from the beach to about a mile inland toward the mountains. The parking areas at the sides of the strip were empty. The only sign of habitation was one footpath crossing a corner of the runway. In two photo runs across the area at four thousand feet, I obtained enough detail to confirm the mission report that I would soon be writing for the intelligence officers.

The weather worsened. I knew I must be heading into a severe front, so I decided to try climbing over it. At eight thousand feet the air was smoother. I leveled off and altered my course to ninety degrees to upset any plot the enemy, using their radar, might have for targeting me. When the clouds began to break up I spotted Lolobau Island glistening in the bright sunlight. This was supposed to be one of Japan's favorite places to hide barges during the daylight hours. I eased back a bit on the throttles and circled the island twice in a fruitless attempt to find signs of enemy activity.

Eight thousand feet was not a safe height to be flying in a clear sky over enemy territory. Turning back to the coast, I started a gradual climb. Maybe it was time to head for home. Off to the right I spotted what looked like the construction of a new airfield. I leveled off and circled the area for a better look. The least I could do was shoot a set of pictures and let the photo interpreters back at the base decide if this was an important find. I carefully lined up for a low-altitude pass over what looked like a runway and set the camera intervelometer for a series of overlapping pictures.

GOODBYE *EAGER BEAVER*

The cameras were rolling when I was startled by a series of sharp staccato sounds. *Eager Beaver* quivered a bit as I made a hurried check of the engine instruments. Everything seemed normal. Suddenly a long jagged tear appeared in the port-engine cowling. An instant later a puff of black smoke shot out from the hole, followed by a burst of flame. Instinctively I sent *Eager Beaver* into a screaming dive with throttles wide open; only then did I dare sneak a glance at the rearview mirror. I was afraid to look—but afraid not to. Turning my head, I stared straight into the flaming snout of a twin-engine enemy fighter.

I felt the plane shudder as a burst of lead ricocheted off the armor plate behind me. For a second I was able to sideslip out of the line of fire. At the same time I cut off the left engine because it was now spitting red flame. I tried to get Beaver under control. She was losing altitude fast! I cast a hopeful eye toward a bank of low clouds to the south, hoping I could hide in them. The right engine died with a loud burp, and so did any hope of seeking cloud cover. The needle on the fuel-pressure gauge began to waver and plopped down to zero. It had all happened in rapid sequence, but it almost seemed that I was watching it unfold in slow motion on a brilliantly lit stage—with myself in the leading role.

My vision blurred and I swiped my hand across my forehead. It came away bloody and I realized I'd been hit—by bullet or shrapnel, I didn't know. My main concern was how to abandon *Beaver*. It was no longer a matter of choice. Bailing out of a P-38 was never supposed to be an option, but I knew if I ever wanted to eat fresh eggs again I'd better figure how to get out under less-than-ideal conditions. I wasn't going to let my time run out without giving it a try. Most pilots agreed that by making a forced landing, the odds for survival went up considerably. There was nothing below that gave me that option. The ground was coming up awfully fast. I needed to jettison the cockpit canopy, so I pulled on the emergency hatch-release handle. The canopy popped partway open but didn't disengage. I unbuckled my seat belt and rose up to have a better look. Socko! A blast of air hit me under the chin and sucked me out of the cockpit as though I had been lassoed. In an instant I was swinging from side to side under the nylon canopy of my parachute.

The training manual was one bit of literature I hadn't read, but evidently I had done everything right—or else my guardian angel was on the job. Then my chute started drifting toward the spot where my plane had crashed in flames. I knew I didn't want to land anywhere near it and began pulling the shroud lines to change direction. The Japanese fighter plane came wheeling around in a screaming dive. I was a sitting duck and figured I'd had it for sure, but for some reason the pilot made no effort to finish me off. I was over enemy-occupied territory, so maybe he thought that his ground troops would capture me, or that I couldn't survive in the jungle. I crashed down through some huge eucalyptus trees—the perfect cover. My time wasn't up yet.

My brain slowly started to function again as the sound of the fighter faded away into the distance. I had been running on adrenalin, but now reality was setting in. I had to put what had happened behind me and go about the business of survival. I picked myself up out of the mud and found that I was intact except for a long gash on my head that was bleeding profusely. The blood had run down my face and neck and seemed to be everywhere. I remembered the parachute sergeant saying that a survival kit was tucked in the back cushion of the chute. I pulled on the zipper and dumped everything out to look for some medicine. The iodine syrettes had dried up. I wondered if they were relics of some previous war. The sulfanilamide tablets were crushed to a powder. I sprinkled some of it on my wound, cut strips from my parachute, made a pad, and held it in place with a clumsily wound bandage—crude but effective.

Inventory revealed that the kit also held a compass, a large machete knife with a razor-sharp edge, a waterproof match box, extra ammunition for my pistol, a fishing line and hooks, penicillin, two bars of chocolate, a canvas water bag, and several sticks of twist tobacco to be used as gifts for any natives that I might encounter. Fastened to the bottom of the chute was a tiny inflatable life raft.

I also uncovered a small booklet entitled *Friendly Fruits and Vegetables: Advice to Air Crew Members Forced Down in the Jungle.* I read fast and furiously. "Above all else," it said, "keep calm." Well, that should be easy—the big excitement was over. The next paragraph cheered me up a little. "The two bars of emergency-ration chocolate should last you for ten days, and by that time you are sure to find friendly natives." Seventy-five miles of thick jungle and two hundred miles of open sea stood between me and my home base, but *Friendly Fruits and Vegetables* made it seem as if it were just over the hill.

My next move was to cut several sections of nylon from my chute to provide cover from the elements. The machete was invaluable, cutting through the straps of the parachute like butter. I figured I could use them to fashion a backpack to carry whatever I needed for survival. I felt ready to cope with anything, but when I ceased my activity I became aware of the deathly silence around me. It was then that the reality of my situation fully sank in. I had never before been that alone in my life. Sounds that I had taken for granted at home were missing here—no hum of traffic in the distance, no children playing, doors slamming, or lawn mowers buzzing. I heard a faint whisper of wind in the canopy of trees above me, and an occasional birdcall. That was it. Were all the jungle creatures aware of me? After all, I was an alien in their world. Part of a Bible quotation came to me. What was it? Something about "no bird falling that He wasn't aware of." I gave myself a mental shake and set out to do what I could. Then another quotation came to mind, something I had heard the family oldsters say: "God helps those who help themselves." My next move was to find shelter.

There were no paths to follow, just a wall of foliage. Compass in hand, I set a course for the mainland of New Guinea and plunged into the bush. It seemed darker than it had been when I crashed; undoubtedly it would be raining shortly. I looked around for a campsite. A level spot under a huge tree appeared promising. Once more I turned to *Friendly Fruits* for guidance. A sketch showed me how to construct a tent from strips of parachute cloth, so I set to work with all the vigor of a Boy Scout earning a merit badge. Rain began to fall about nine o'clock and the tent worked exactly as the booklet promised. "This type of shelter," it said, "will not be absolutely waterproof, but if constructed properly it should afford ample protection from severe storms." If properly constructed—hah! I spent the rest of the night dodging streams of water pouring through the roof. A few times I drifted off to sleep and dreamed I was home in bed, only to be jerked awake by the throbbing pain in my head.

I began to make a mental list of things I needed. A guide and a canoe loomed large in my thoughts, soon to be replaced by something less serious. I wondered if anyone would water the zinnias in my victory garden back in camp. Thinking about flowers while slogging through the jungle didn't seem at all incongruous.

Those zinnias reminded me of home—that's why I had planted them.

Next my mind was filled with fantastic escape schemes. Maybe I could get to a nearby airdrome and steal a Zero. Or perhaps I could signal friendly aircraft and be picked up by a flying boat. Finally I decided I would have to find a native and go back to New Guinea in a canoe. Yes, yes, find a native. That was the most important step. Didn't *Friendly Fruits* say I should make contact with one within the next ten days? It was a comforting thought, but would I find the natives or would they find me?

By the next morning my head had stopped bleeding, but I was suffering from the effects of my unfamiliar living conditions and the trauma of being shot down by enemy fire. I sucked on a tiny square of emergency chocolate, trying to keep the taste in my mouth as long as possible. A lizard dashed across the front of my tent and vanished into the bushes before I could get my pistol out of the holster. But if I were lucky enough to kill one, how would I prepare it? It was plain that even though I might know how survive on my home turf, I was a lowly tenderfoot out here in the jungle. Soon movement in the top of a nearby tree caught my eye. A lone cockatoo stretched its wings in the first light of the morning sun. It was a beautiful sight, but I could have savored it more had I not been worrying about more important things—such as finding food and getting home.

The mosquitoes weren't bad and I was thankful for that, but insects of another sort made my life miserable. They were everywhere—slow-flying, soft-bodied critters determined to invade every orifice. I was continually brushing them away from my eyes, nose, and mouth. There was no end to them—kill one and it would be replaced by two, four, a dozen. They seemed to multiply in midair. They were smaller than flies and larger than gnats, but I called them gnats for lack of proper identification.

It was time to get moving. I wrapped the articles from the jungle kit in the parachute, checked directions with the compass, and started out. The air was cool and damp, and the jungle foliage was still wet from the night's rain. Each time I brushed against a tree or bush I got a cold shower. At midday the drone of an approaching plane broke the silence. Hoping it might be someone from my squadron out searching for me, I rushed to a clear spot. The plane was almost overhead when I saw the two red spots on the silver wings—the Japanese rising sun! Quickly I stepped back out of sight.

Traveling was getting tougher all the time. After spending the entire afternoon trying to pull myself up the side of a steep ravine, I decided to abandon the idea of holding a compass course. I knew that if I followed a stream I would eventually reach the ocean and perhaps a native village.

Finding a stream was no problem; I was surrounded by them. Following it was another matter. Actually, I was *in* it most of the time. The dense growth along the bank forced me to wade. My heavy Aussie flying boots quickly filled with water and weighed me down. I knew I wouldn't have much reserve strength until I got some decent food under my belt, so I took the boots off, tied them together, and carried them over my shoulder. It didn't help much, though, because my feet slipped on the moss-covered rocks. Over and over again I went crashing down into the water. I would get up, try to find something solid under my feet, take few steps—and down I'd go again. My calmness got eroded a little bit more each time it happened, until finally it had completely evaporated. I was just plain mad. By nightfall I was so tired I couldn't even swear.

I allowed myself to savor another square of chocolate for supper before turning to *Friendly Fruits* to see what kind of fauna or flora I might expect to find. "If you are on the coast," it said, "you should find plenty of fruit, especially bananas. If they are green, roast them in a fire. If you are in northern Australia, try building a signal fire and you will probably be picked up by friendly aborigines." I felt a little grim. Anyone downed outside of those parameters was on his own. I was at least 150 miles from the coast and 1,500 miles from northern Australia.

A search along the banks of the stream finally produced a lily-shaped plant that the booklet described as wild taro. According to the directions, I was supposed to place the bulbous root in the fire. Ah, the fire! I had yet to build one. Should I attempt it when my supply of matches was so limited? I decided to scratch the idea until I reached a better environment.

I kept searching for a way out of the dense jungle. Each time I discovered what I thought was a viable path, it would disappear into a maze of tangled vines and fallen trees. The huge logs were so decayed that when I sat on them to rest, they usually crumbled into powder and disgorged scores of big red ants. As a kid I had enjoyed the story of Robinson Crusoe's adventures, but living them was something else. The novelty was wearing thin. I had never thought I would see the day when GI fare would be not only acceptable, but also welcome. I didn't actually dream about eating bully beef, powdered eggs, dehydrated potatoes, and powdered milk—but they were often in my thoughts.

To keep my mind occupied, I daydreamed about my days at Iowa State College. The campus had buildings covered with vines, but not the choking, all-consuming kind that filled the jungle. Back in those days I had told myself that if war ever came, I would pack up a load of food and camp for the duration on some secluded island in the middle of a northern Minnesota lake. Now fate was grinning at me. Leering was a better word for it. I'd probably be here for the duration all right, but this wasn't Minnesota, and the food supply that seemed such a minor concern back at college was missing. I kicked that idea around for a while and realized that new circumstances can certainly bring a new attitude—not only about the moment, but also about life in general.

On the tenth day my hopes rose when I discovered what seemed to be a well-traveled path. It led to a high bluff along the river, dropped to water level, and finally broke out before a native lean-to. Freshly cut kunai grass covered the roof. Even more heartening were signs of recent cuttings on the nearby trees. Maybe *Friendly Fruits* was right after all.

With my shelter problem solved for the time being, my thoughts turned to building a fire. After gathering what dry wood I could find, I opened the waterproof box and counted the ten matches. It seemed they would be more than enough. I struck the first one and waited expectantly for the flame to catch on my little pile of wood. No luck! The next six matches flared up and died with no better success. I counted the three remaining matches. My chances of survival pretty much depended on them. I rearranged the twigs in teepee fashion and struck another match. A gust of wind caught the flame as it danced on the tip of the match, blowing it out. I wanted to kick myself for being so inept. Cautiously I struck the next-to-last match. It flashed and fizzled out—a dud. It seemed impossible that nine matches had failed to start a fire. I began to panic. Should I use the last match or wait for a really dry day?

Why hadn't I thought of it before? The twists of tobacco were wrapped in newspaper. I tore open my escape kit and carefully placed a crumpled piece of the *New York Daily Sentinel* into the center of the woodpile and knelt down for one last try. The paper burst into flame. A few breathless seconds later the wood caught fire. My heartbeat slowed to normal as I gave an inner shout of joy and thanksgiving. It was amazing how that little blaze lifted my spirits. The sight of flames flickering in the wood, the snap and crackle and even the smell of smoke appealed to my senses and assured me that I was back in business.

While investigating my new homestead, I uncovered some small shells in an old fire bed. Referring to *Friendly Fruits*, now back in my good graces, I read that snails living in the moss along rocky fresh-water streams were easy to find and very nourishing. The rapids in front of my lean-to harbored a veritable bonanza of them. I harvested two huge fistfuls, carried them back in triumph, and roasted them on a few coals at the edge of the fire. Before long I found I could extract the meat with the tip of my knife. I also learned to season the delectable bits by holding part of a salt tablet in the back of my mouth while I ate. I thought of the guys back at the base eating bully beef and biscuits, while my own limited menu was second only to caviar.

That night I went to bed with my belly full of snails. It was a peculiar night. I counted snails instead of sheep, then dreamed they were crawling around my insides and sticking out my ears. My diet for the next three weeks, morning, noon and night, would be more of the same, but that didn't keep me from enjoying them. I just wished I had some garlic butter.

As I settled in, I began to pay more attention to my surroundings. My hunger made me notice something else I could add to the menu: two spotted fish darting in and around the rocks where I got my drinking water. First I tried to snare them with a net I had fashioned from strips of parachute nylon. Then I made a trident-like spear from a sapling by tying a three-pointed stick to one end. The fish, however, were too clever—or I was too slow. That night I tried to lure them to the surface by burning a bark torch. I remembered that back home some of the old boys who didn't want to work too hard at fishing used torches to lure catfish right up to the bank. But these weren't catfish and my effort was futile. Evidently these fish weren't going to take anything but a genuine, skillfully cast lure.

I gave up on the idea of a fish dinner until one morning a grasshopper hopped across the floor of my shelter and landed on a blade of tall grass. Here was a lure, made to order. I remembered how Pop had used local bugs when he fished the streams and lakes of Minnesota. The South Bend Bait Company couldn't have come up with anything better than that grasshopper. The problem was, I was counting on a fish dinner before I had the lure in hand. The grasshopper was as clever as the fish. I stalked him around the hut for what seemed like hours, but each time I thought I had him cornered, he gave a mighty leap and landed out of reach. Finally he came to rest on a log.

It was my move. I froze like a hunting dog on point. Slowly I slid my hand forward a scant inch at a time. Eighteen inches more to go; they seemed like eighteen feet. I practically held my breath as two beady back eyes gleaming from an armor-plated head stared up at me. The green jungle-camouflaged body settled back on its haunches. Then, faster than my eye could follow, his legs snapped out, catapulting him over my head in a sweeping arc. Before I could turn my head to follow his passage, there was a whir of wings and the jungle had swallowed him up. My fish dinner was as far away as ever. Disappointment wasn't the only emotion I felt. Being thwarted by a creature so low on the food chain did nothing to bolster my ego, but I consoled myself with the thought that the instinct for survival was in all living things, even a grasshopper.

Coming back from a swim later that day, I spied the grasshopper again. He was perched on the tip of a bamboo stalk, swaying in the light breeze and apparently unaware of my presence. I approached him from behind, pausing after each step to gauge the distance between us. Then with great determination and all the speed I could muster, I made a sweeping grab and closed my fist around him. He was mine! I could feel his legs thrusting against my hand as he struggled to escape. I relaxed my grip enough to let his head wriggle through my thumb and forefinger. He squirmed and heaved as I attempted to thrust the hook through his body. It seemed a cruel thing to do, but visions of a fish dinner overcame my qualms.

I failed to get so much as a nibble with him that day, so in the evening I propped the pole up with rocks, hoping a hungry fish would grab the bait overnight and become my breakfast. The next morning I was up at dawn to haul in my expected catch. My heart plummeted when I discovered both hook and line had been carried away. A few minutes later I spied one of the fish swimming around. I imagined that he had a "cat-that-ate-the-canary" look on his face. That made me more than a little upset. Mad was the word for it. I ran to the hut and grabbed my pistol. Crawling up to the edge of the bank, I spotted him in shallow water. Taking careful aim and allowing for the distortion of the water, I fired. A geyser of water shot up. As the surface cleared, I saw the fish lying on his side on the bottom of the pool. My shot hadn't hit him, but he was stunned by the force of the bullet's passage through the water. I saw his tail quiver a little, so (fearing he might come to and escape again) I dropped the pistol on the bank and scrambled, clothes and all, into the water to get my breakfast.

I gathered some large leaves to serve as a plate, split him open with the machete, cleaned him out, seasoned him with a mashed salt tablet, then spitted him on a green stick propped above the coals. I had earned that fish and enjoyed every bite of him.

Finding food was a minor problem compared to the diligence it took to keep my fire going day and night. More than once I would awaken to find only a tiny ember glowing, and would practically hyperventilate as I blew and blew to bring it back to life. One day while searching for berries to supplement my diet of snails, some sixth sense warned me to return to camp at once. I raced back, hoping to see a trace of smoke through the trees. Panic added a bit more speed to my pace. "Oh God," I pleaded, "don't let the fire go out."

Another turn in the trail and I reached camp. No smoke, nothing. The fire bed was as cold as a gravestone. How could I have let my inattention destroy my most comforting means of survival? It was my very life. I squatted at the edge of the pile of ashes, filled with despair. I couldn't eat the snails raw. The fire was also a guard against intruders and seemed almost like a living companion. Was my escape from the P-38 merely a reprieve, leading to a worse death from starvation? I poked the ashes with a stick. A little puff of smoke arose. Down on my knees now, I brushed the ashes away and uncovered a live ember. Mentally I caressed it with a blessing. It began to glow faintly, so I quickly rustled up some dry twigs and bark shavings. In a few minutes my fire was going again. That experience left me with a thorough understanding of why people had worshipped fire, but I didn't say my thanks to an ancient fire god.

What came to my lips was a prayer dredged up from my days as a child in Sunday School, said with more heartfelt understanding than I had ever experienced before. "The Lord is my shepherd, I shall not want..." The words came easily and I finished the psalm, feeling humble, thankful, and strengthened.

My survival meant an almost constant search for food, which kept my mind occupied during the day. The nights were a different story. I dreaded them, but not because I feared animal intruders. It was the dreams that haunted me. Weeks had passed since I had bailed out of *Eager Beaver*, but the trauma continued to grip me. I had terrifying nightmares, sometimes about those moments when I struggled to escape from the cockpit, and other times about the even more terrifying prospect of dying alone in the jungle.

The long days of lonely existence had begun to take their toll. Friendly faces were three hundred miles away, and my family was thousands of miles away in the middle of my homeland. That word, *home*, took on many new meanings. It was family, friends, security, future...even the extremes of weather. I thought of cold, snow, ice—and, strange as it seemed there in the steaming jungle, I even missed Minnesota's brand of hot, lazy summers.

Occasionally I would find myself humming a Phi Delta Theta drinking song. It wasn't that I needed a drink; that had never been important to me. But the song brought back pleasant memories and the faces of my fraternity brothers as we gathered around the dinner table in the evenings. It also gave me a reason to use my vocal cords. Would they atrophy from disuse? I prayed I'd have a joyous reason to use them again.

After a month in the jungle, I admitted to myself that I was tired and hungry. It was obvious that I had lost weight. I looked like a scarecrow in the tattered clothes that hung loosely on my bony frame. My greatest misery, however, was summed up in one simple sentence: I was alone.

A DAY LIKE ALL THE REST

July 6 was a day like all the rest: a morning swim, a hike in the bush to hunt for dry wood, roasted snails for lunch, and an afternoon nap. Just before sunset I took off my clothes and went to the edge of the river to gather bamboo shoots for supper. I was aware of vitamins and my need for vegetable greens. I knew I probably wouldn't die of loneliness, but I could die of scurvy. That thought compelled me to try anything I could find that *Friendly Fruits* suggested.

A few minutes into my search for the shoots, I was startled by what seemed to be voices coming from downstream. Could they be real, or was I hallucinating? I wasn't going to jump to conclusions, but the sound grew in volume. It might have been just the water burbling over the rocky streambed—that had fooled me before. I cocked my ear toward the ever-increasing sound. Finally the slender nose of an outrigger canoe pushed into view from behind a clump of trees that flanked the near side of the stream. It was followed by a crowd of natives chatting and singing as they waded through the shallow water.

My first impulse was to run into the bushes and hide, at least until I could find out whether or not they were friendly. But my feet were glued to the ground. I couldn't move an inch. Suddenly a tremendous shout arose as the natives spotted my naked figure crouched in the tall bamboo grasses. I had no choice now; escape was out of the question. As the natives approached, their talk was an unintelligible babble to me. I strained my ears, hoping to hear something identifiable. Then I thought I heard one of them yell, "*Masta, Masta, you nambawan!*" I wondered what he meant. Was I a number-one friend, or number one for the soup pot? I recalled an intelligence officer's briefing before I took off on the mission. "If you get into trouble over New Britain, stay away from the beach. Japanese soldiers are known to be making daily patrols along the coast. Going too far into the mountains could be risky as well. We've had reports that a warlike tribe of Makolkol headhunters has been making night raids on villages to collect their trophies."

A wiry, dark-skinned man with short curly hair stepped forward. Spokesman or chief, it didn't matter. I tried to remember the native words in *Friendly Fruits* but my mind was a complete blank. Fortunately, even in my state of suspended animation I could see that there was no iron kettle in their canoe.

Finally my brain made a connection to my feet and I screwed up enough courage to start walking towards the canoe. I moved cautiously, wondering if these people had been sent out by the Japanese to look for me—one big trophy for them. The man I had picked out as the leader or elder of the group came closer. I looked straight into his deep-set eyes, hoping for some friendly sign. I wasn't watching where I was going and nearly fell as I stubbed my toe on a partially exposed rock. The elder reached out a strong arm to steady me. All my fears vanished as I saw a warm and sympathetic smile spread across his face.

"You numba-one fellow too," I croaked. My first words to another human being in thirty-one days! He grinned excitedly and shook my hand. Seconds later, the strong arm of another native was steadying me. Then yet another man rushed up, waving a notebook. Scribbled on the second page was a note that read, "To Whomever it May Concern. The bearer of this letter, Luluai Lauo, has proven his loyalty to the Allied Forces by assisting in the rescue of three American airmen who were shot down by the Japanese. These natives can be trusted, and anyone finding himself in similar circumstances will receive good food and care. John Stokie, A.I.F."

Before I had even finished reading, tears began to trickle down my cheeks. My prayers had been answered. I was about to be overcome by emotion when suddenly I realized I was standing there without a stitch of clothing on. I hadn't noticed the girls who were sitting modestly in the rear of the canoe until they all started giggling. I was sure nudity was nothing new to them, but it was to me. Hoping to salvage what dignity I could muster, I hurried to the lean-to and slipped into my tattered trousers. When I reappeared, the canoe had been pulled ashore and the troupe gathered around me for a closer look. I felt like a shaggy, ungroomed poodle at a dog show. I had a month-old beard and my hair was hanging down on my neck—a far cry from the dapper airman who had taken off in *Eager Beaver* thirty-one days earlier.

Friendly Fruits had a section called "Conversation With Natives," but each of my questions brought the same reply. "*Sori Masta, mi no savi.*" (*Masta* was the way they addressed all ex-patriate men—a tradition left over from the early 1900s, when Germans owned many of the local plantations. Since independence, it—along with *Misis* for expatriate women—had lost any "master-servant" connotations and become simply a polite form of identification, much like "Mister.")

I finally recalled a lecture on jungle survival from a class at the squadron's air base. The lecturer had advised trying simple English words if the natives failed to understand what was in the jungle guidebooks.

"Japan, he stop?" I queried.

The elder shook his head. "*No gat. Ol Japan em i go pinis taim bepo.*"

I took that to mean that the Japanese had left. Then, following the advice in what I now thought of as both bible and encyclopedia, I reached into my pocket and passed out a few Australian coins. This brought more friendly smiles. Feeling better all the time, I pointed to my stomach and gave an empty look.

"*Masta, em i laik kisim kaikai? I gat bikpela hangre?*"

I nodded. "Me hungry plenty."

Things were certainly picking up. The elder rattled off a long speech that I didn't understand while two little boys ran down to the canoe. They returned with a basket of bananas, pineapples, sweet potatoes, taro, smoked fish, and a chunk of roast pig. Then a terrible thing happened. I reacted like some little kid with a huge plate of food set before him. In the face of plenty, my appetite fled. My desperate need to survive had supported me for a whole month, and now the excitement of the moment overcame my hunger.

One man had the words "Joseph Gabu" tattooed across his chest. When I called him by this name, his face lit up and a smile flickered at the corner of his mouth. From that moment on we were strong friends.

Gabu was an admirable man. When someone discovered that my fire, which had burned continuously for twenty days, had finally died, he simply shrugged his shoulders, produced a couple of dry sticks from his basket, and began rubbing them together. When a tiny curl of smoke drifted up, he knelt down and blew life into the single spark. Then he carefully added some dry bark shavings and blew some more Smoke poured out and within a second the whole pile of twigs and bark burst into flame. I was humbled, to say the least.

Sleep eluded me that first night. I felt like a kid on Christmas Eve. I lay awake in my hut listening to the singing and chanting of the natives, feeling very good about being a member of the human family again. Once in awhile I thought I could detect bits of melody taken from church hymns. I might have imagined it, but the effect was pleasing. Clearly, raising their voices in song was as an important part of village life.

Wisps of fog were still clinging to the trees along the river in the morning when the natives began to break camp in preparation for the trek downstream. Somebody brought me a billy-tin of hot fish stew, but the excitement of my now-improved situation, not to mention the prospect of joining my squadron, sublimated my desire for food. Reasoning that the natives would have some way of signaling a plane, I wanted to be on my way. I thought if word that I was alive reached Port Moresby, headquarters would send a Catalina flying boat for me.

My immediate transportation, however, was the outrigger canoe. It was hand-carved from a long log that was at least four feet in diameter. For stability, a long pole lay in the water along one side, parallel to the craft and attached to it with several smaller poles. It looked too flimsy to be seaworthy, but I remembered seeing similar boats carrying natives up and down the coast near Port Moresby.

Three heavy planks had been placed across the center of the outrigger to make a platform. It was there I was to sit, sightsee, and sleep until we reached the coast. With one man poling in the bow position and another pushing from the stern, we eased into the middle of the river, where a strong current reached out and began sweeping us along quite rapidly. Any doubts I had about the safety of the craft proved groundless. The natives were skillful oarsmen, picking safe passage through rapids and swirling currents.

They were also very much aware of their surroundings, including the sky above. Whenever we heard the sound of an approaching plane, one of them would sing out, *"Balus!"* The rest would pick up the cry. *"Balus, balus bilong Japan!"* There would be a scramble while Gabu shouted orders and the canoe headed for the side of the river, seeking protection under the overhang of vegetation. They believed that the *man bilong balus* with his *glas lukluk* could observe every movement on the ground unless it was hidden in the bush.

At noon we pulled into a small tributary. Armed with a heavy spear, Gabu climbed out onto the bank to hunt for *bolo*. In a few minutes we heard a loud rustle in the bushes and Luluai (Chief) Lauo yelled, *"Bolo, bolo."* A terrified squeal filled the air. There was the thud of pounding feet and then dead silence. Soon Gabu broke through the underbrush, leading two other natives who were carrying a huge wild pig suspended on a pole between them. Blood dripped from a gaping hole in the pig's side where Gabu's spear had struck. I looked anxiously at the vines binding his legs as the natives dumped him, still struggling violently, into the front of the canoe. The rest of the party was jubilant.

The river widened and deepened and I sensed we were nearing the sea. Occasionally I got a whiff of salt air, clearly distinct from the dank jungle atmosphere. As we rounded a bend, I spotted a sprawling garden that sloped down to the water's edge. Two children, wading in the shallows, waved and then scurried up the bank. Several half-naked women straightened up from their labors in a patch of sugar cane and spoke in high-pitched voices. Gabu exchanged some words with them. Immediately they got into another canoe and moved out ahead of us. I later learned that they served as point guards, keeping an eye out for any hostile tribesmen or Japanese patrols. Our own outrigger stopped in a quiet pool to await the "all clear" signal. In a few minutes the voices of the women in the second canoe came back over the water. The coast was clear and we landed.

The village of Ae Ae (now called Nantabu) was a cluster of little grass-covered lean-tos at the edge of a lagoon near the river. A crowd of excited natives rushed down to the water to help beach the outrigger. I had barely stepped ashore when they began shaking my hand. They evidently considered it a privilege to greet me, although some of the more timid girls had to be coaxed before they would come near. Nursing mothers held out their babies for me to touch.

Luluai Lauo led me to his hut, where a special bed had been prepared for me. Constructed of three planks on two cross-pieces, it was supported by forked sticks driven into the ground. Lauo proudly described it as *gutpela tumas* ("good fellow too much"—very good!). Everyone waited expectantly for my response. I mustered a smile of thanks, but that night my bones nearly poked through my skin. Adding to my insomnia was the presence of eight other people in the house. It was togetherness to the nth degree—the luluai, his wife, and her six cousins. When they weren't talking, they were either snoring or grunting.

In the morning I tried to explain that I would like to sleep on the sand, native-style, but Lauo said it was beneath the dignity of a white man to touch the ground with his body. Fortunately, some of his assistants understood that I needed something more forgiving than those hard planks. They gathered some slender boughs that gave a little with every movement, and after that I was more comfortable.

Over the next few days my appetite gradually returned and I feasted on several native dishes. Their staple was taro but not the wild stuff that was so terribly bitter. These cultivated taro roots were shaped like large turnips and tasted something like potatoes. I also had chunks of wild pig and fish seasoned with seawater. The natives would simply throw a cupful or two of seawater into the boiling pot. It didn't take me long to tire of boiled pig, but when I asked for some of their juicy roasted pig, they insisted it was not good for me. When I finally talked them into letting me try it, I got an intestinal ailment from which I have never fully recovered. Was there something toxic in the fat that boiling removed? I never ate it again.

Luluai Lauo was often called in for questioning by the Japanese garrison, located about eight miles down the coast. Whenever this happened, I spent an anxious day wondering if he would inform on me. But his loyalty was steadfast. On some of these trips he would carry a basket of fruit or vegetables to trade for cigarettes, quinine, or an occasional bag of rice. Most of the time, however, he returned empty-handed.

Enemy patrols began to appear more frequently along the beach, so Lauo had a small concealed hut built for me in a nearby swamp. I often hid there during the day, and villagers were stationed along the shore to warn of Japanese or hostile natives. Unless I happened to be barefoot, two children always followed behind me to cover my bootprints. When I came out of hiding at night, I sat around the fire chatting with the villagers. This turned out to be an excellent way to learn New Guinea Pidgin, the lingua franca of Papua New Guinea.

During every full moon we tried to signal the four-engine bombers that flew the night skies on their way to strike enemy ships in the harbor at Rabaul. Three natives would stand at ten-yard intervals along the beach, each waving a torch made from dried coconut leaves. None of the planes seemed to notice our signs—or if they did, they must have thought it was a Japanese ruse of some sort. Several minutes later the long fingers of enemy searchlights would pierce the sky, and the thud of exploding bombs would rumble across the bay.

One day while I was back up the river working in the garden, the luluai's wife came running up to me, screaming that a party of Japanese soldiers was approaching the village. Gabu grabbed me and we ran deep into the jungle. I carried my boots over my shoulder to avoid leaving tracks. When we were a safe distance from the garden, Gabu pointed to a vine-choked eucalyptus tree and told me to climb it and hide. At the top I found a mossy nest that had evidently been the sleeping place of some animal. Except for the swarms of mosquitoes that soon zeroed in on me, it was a perfect hideout. (Mosquitoes obviously preferred these coastal areas to the higher elevation where I had spent my month alone.) Gabu shouted that I was to answer only to the call of "*Predi*" (Freddie).

Gabu left and I waited and waited. At times I thought I heard voices in the distance, but I was afraid to move around for fear it was a Japanese patrol. The sun lowered and, as happens in those latitudes, there was no twilight—just sudden darkness. I began to fear I might have to spend the whole night in that nest, and hoped the owner wouldn't show up to claim it. My tangible misery was the viciously persistent mosquitoes, but I dared not start down until I heard the agreed-upon signal. Meanwhile the voices got louder and, wishful thinking or not, I thought I heard someone yell "*Predi.*"

Taking a chance, I shouted at the top of my lungs. There was a scurry of running feet and then shuffling under the tree. I broke into a cold sweat, fearing I had led the enemy to my lair. Then I recognized Gabu's voice among the babble of sound. He was as breathless as I was. After I had clambered down, he apologetically explained that the reason he had taken so long to return was that he couldn't find the tree where he had hidden me! Turned out the Japanese patrol had pushed on long before.

A few weeks later I was seized by a terrible chill that made me shake until my teeth clattered. At first I thought it was an attack of indigestion, but I knew that goose bumps weren't a symptom of that condition. Then the fever hit me, and I prayed the chills would return to cool me off. Breathing was painful and great beads of sweat dripped from my body. When the fever broke many hours later, I was utterly exhausted. I felt as if I had run a marathon. I fell asleep that night in spite of an empty stomach because I was truly too tired to eat.

The next morning I awakened feeling restored and in high spirits. Gabu fixed me a breakfast of fish and boiled rice, which I devoured like a starved puppy. At noon the same icy chills swept over me again. Gabu said, "*Masta em i gat kol sik.*" I had no idea what he was talking about, but each day I went through the same thing—chills and violent shaking followed by fever and profuse sweating. Later I found out I had malaria.

After ten days I was so weak and short-winded that I couldn't move from my bed. I wasn't eating anything. My only nourishment came from reading short passages in the Bible and listening to Apelis Tagogo, a native missionary, and his religious brethren chanting their songs and prayers around my bed.

More days passed and it was obvious I needed something besides prayers and songs. I hadn't eaten for over ten days. When I asked Lauo if he knew where I could get some milk, he sent someone to steal a goat from a plantation near Rabaul. Unfortunately the would-be thief returned empty-handed, saying it was too risky with the Japanese around. Apelis, who was so sympathetic and so anxious to do anything to help me, was heartbroken when he heard the news.

Then Apelis asked, "*Em i kan kaikai susu?*" I wasn't sure what he meant by *susu* but managed a feeble nod. The missionary smiled and raced off toward the village. A couple of hours later he returned, bringing his wife Ida and their month-old baby. She trailed modestly behind him, gazing open-mouthed at me. Apelis handed her a teacup and she stepped behind the grass wall of my hut. A few minutes later she passed the cup back to her husband. Only then did I realize that *susu* was mother's milk. My extreme hunger overcame my embarrassment and any thought of refusing. My benefactors regarded me apprehensively as I put the cup to my lips. One sip and I smiled at Apelis and Ida. Together they nodded and returned my smile.

Every day for the next ten days, Ida supplied me with a small cup of her milk. By the end of the first week I was able to eat a little fruit and could manage to sit up in bed for a few minutes. Gradually the alternating chills and fever vanished, and finally I could take a few steps. Each day I gained strength and added a few more halting steps. I knew then that my *kol sik* (cold-sickness) had run its course.

Just when I was finally eating more or less normally, I was beset by something new—a severe case of diarrhea. When native remedies failed to help, Quali, one of the villagers, offered to take a note to the "padre" asking if he had a cure for my ailment. According to Quali, at the start of hostilities a German Catholic missionary and four lay brothers had left their mission station on the coast and retreated into the hills. The Japanese had evidently decided to ignore them, so they lived in their cloister unmolested. A letter could be delivered to the padre without anyone else knowing. Luluai Lauo was not sure that he could read English, however, since the "*padre bilong Germany.*" I wrote a note in simple English, explaining my illness, and then added a few German phrases I remembered from school. I mentioned that "mein grossfater vas apotica [druggist] in Duesseldorf," hoping that would be enough to prompt the good padre to send the medicine I needed.

Three days later Quali rushed into my hut, wearing a wide grin on his face. He carried a small parcel wrapped with banana leaves and tied with vines. Inside were two leaf-wrapped packages. One contained a tiny vial of dark liquid. Since I couldn't read the Oriental characters printed on its green paper label, there was no way to tell whether it was for diarrhea or constipation. The second bottle was a glass cylinder of Dr. Morse's Indian Root Pills—exactly like the ones sold over the counter at Pop's drugstore. They were touted to be good for the liver and a general cure-all. Since they were also good for constipation, I knew that the tiny vial probably contained paregoric. When I opened it, a sniff confirmed that deduction and I swallowed it all. By the end of the day my diarrhea was gone.

A few days later I took several doses of the Indian Root Pills just for good measure. They must have had curative powers of some sort, because the next day I was able to move from my bed. With the help of a cane I walked to a nearby stream for a bath. It was good to wash the smell of sickness from my thinner-than-thin body.

Many times low-flying planes circled the village. I always took cover until I was sure they were friendly, but by then they were flying away. One morning while we were standing on the beach watching the sunrise, Luluai Lauo pointed out a tiny speck in the direction of Rabaul. It came nearer and nearer and I assumed it was a Japanese plane on morning patrol. A few seconds later I recognized the silhouette of a Douglass A-20. I grabbed a shirt from one of the natives and waved it back and forth. Just as the plane reached the village, it turned in a steep bank to circle the little island offshore where Japanese barges had been hiding. The maneuver exposed the belly of the plane and cut me off from the pilot's view. My spirits plummeted. I handed the fellow his shirt and turned away.

One morning the grapevine brought the alarming news that hostile natives were leading a Japanese patrol our way to investigate a rumor that an American aviator was hiding in one of the villages. Probably one of those unfriendly natives had spied me taking a swim and hurried to relay the information to a Japanese officer. The situation was precarious to say the least. If the Japanese threatened to torture any of the local tribesmen, my freedom would be short-lived. Lauo, Gabu, and I got into a huddle and decided that someone should take me far up the river until the enemy patrol left. When the patrol arrived in the village, Lauo would give them some doubletalk and send them on their way.

When we were about to leave, the luluai called his people together and gave them a talk about loyalty to the allied forces. *"Sapos Oli Japan, liak painim Masta Predi, yu no kan tok. Yu mas pas em dispela samting long beli bilong yupela."* (In other words, if any Japanese came, no one had seen me. My whereabouts were to be kept a secret inside their stomachs.) *"Dispela samting,"* he continued. *"Em i wok bilong gavmen. Bihain, ol boi kan kisim bikpela peim."* (The job of hiding me was the same as working for the government, and later they would all be rewarded for doing a good job.)

Lauo assigned a bodyguard to take me to a safe place up the river. We kept pretty close to the riverbank. Occasionally we would cross back and forth and sometimes wade for a while to confuse anyone who might be following us. We came to a small island where the river split into two branches. The swift current made it impossible for anyone to approach quietly. It looked like a perfect hideout. We waded through the rocky places and swam across the deep stretches until finally we stepped ashore and were immediately swallowed up by the tall kunai grass.

The night passed without incident. It was difficult for me to be inactive, and by noon the next day my patience was wearing thin. Finally, a conscious attempt to relax bore fruit and I dozed off. Suddenly my guide nudged me and whispered that the enemy patrol had arrived. My heart skipped a beat when I heard voices coming from the opposite shore. They were too far away to be easily understood, but they did seem to be arguing about whether or not to cross the river. I was prepared to make a dash for the other side when I heard Gabu's voice telling someone that the river was too swift there.

We heard a splash followed by more arguing. Then the voices slowly faded away. I took a deep breath and felt my pulse drop to normal. It seemed I was forever living on the edge. Once more the natives had kept me from falling off.

The next day we arrived back at the village and learned that the Japanese had threatened to execute Gabu if he didn't lead them to my hiding place. Gabu, however, had thwarted them by following my trail to the edge of the river and then insisting that it was too dangerous to go across.

Several days later a native bounded into my hut. With great excitement he began talking so rapidly that I couldn't understand a word. For a heart-stopping moment I thought there was another Japanese patrol in the neighborhood, but Gabu appeared with two more natives. One of them he introduced as "*Sakova, boi bilong Masta Stokie.*"

Sakova appeared to be from a different tribe. He was well-put-together—wiry, strong, and vigorous. Two narrow bracelets, braided from some sort of yellow fibers or grasses, encircled his biceps. A long scar stretched across one arm, evidence that he had been in some sort of knife-wielding fray. Reaching into a small wicker basket that hung from one shoulder, he pulled out a letter and handed it to me. Addressed to the Airman at Ae Ae, it said that if I returned with the bearer, I would find friends. It was signed by Captain Ian Skinner, A.I.F.

I thought our forces must have landed on the other side of the island, and that this was an advance patrol. My whole body trembled with excitement as I shouted to the natives, "*Soldia bilong mipela em i kamap nau—gutpela tumas!*" ("Soldiers of mine are coming—a good feeling!")

Sakova, however, seemed tense, and I felt he was holding something back. He was unwilling to say where the soldiers were, or why they had come to the island. He was afraid that gossip or loose talk might get back to the Japanese. I finally asked everyone to leave the hut, and then he told me the rest of the story.

Sakova said that Stokie and two other Australians were back in the hills with a "wireless." They had been brought to the island by boat, under cover of darkness. He showed me the .45 pistol he carried as protection against unfriendly natives, and told of a trip to Port Moresby where he had seen *planti tumas balus, olsem gras* (many airplanes, like many blades of grass).

After a bit I called Lauo into the hut. I told him I wanted to go back with Sakova, but he thought that in my condition the trip would be too difficult. He suggested I send a letter instead, so I scratched a message to Stokie explaining that I was too sick to attempt such a trek now, but that I would try to come later if I could get some quinine. Sakova's legs were *tait tumas* (very tight), so another runner was sent in his place.

Three days passed with no response to my message. I was so impatient and so desperate for something to happen that I persuaded the luluai to let someone take me to the river so I could wait for the returning messenger. At nightfall we set out by canoe, arriving at the mouth of the river by sunrise. We stopped long enough to load up some fruits and vegetables and then resumed paddling.

COASTWATCHERS

About noon I spotted a cardboard container floating in the water. The natives broke into a hurried conversation as a canoe rounded a bend in the river about two hundred yards away. We couldn't make out any faces, but one of the party was wearing an Australian campaign hat. I let out a yell and nearly upset the canoe as I stood up to wave.

In another moment we had beached our canoe on a sandbar. When I stepped out, the first white man I'd seen in five months quickly came forward and introduced himself as Captain Ian Skinner of the Australian Infantry. He carried a carbine over his shoulder and wore short khaki pants with knee-length stockings. After asking the natives to build a fire, he offered me a cigarette and a spot of tea.

I bombarded him with questions. What was his mission on the island? Did he think I could be rescued? How was the battle for New Guinea going?

Captain Skinner was the OIC (Officer-in-Charge) of an Australian Coastwatchers[1] operation. Their main role was to gather

---

[1] The Coastwatchers was an organization of some four hundred personnel who operated a chain of radio-equipped posts in New Guinea and Australia. Their principal role was to warn the allied forces of Japanese shipping, aircraft, and troop movements. Sixty percent of their members came from the Royal Australian Navy and Army. Men from the Royal Australian Air Force, the New Zealand Navy, the British Solomon Islands Protectorate Defense Force, the Dutch Army, and the U.S. Army and Marine Corps also belonged, as did civilians from New Guinea and elsewhere.

In order to perform their hazardous duties, often from behind enemy lines, the Coastwatchers had to survive under tropical conditions, elude the Japanese, and, in many cases, convince the natives not only that the allies would win the war, but also that the Australians would return to New Guinea. That was not an easy task, considering the fact that the Japanese had become ruthless occupiers of New Guinea after the majority of Australian civilians fled in 1942. The loyalty of the indigenous population was extremely important to the survival of individual Coastwatchers, to the success of their whole operation, and ultimately to the outcome and early end of the war in that theater.

Forty-five Coastwatchers were killed, including twenty members of the native troops and sixteen out of the eighteen members who were taken prisoner by the Japanese. Weighed against these losses was the priceless intelligence they gathered— intelligence that resulted in the destruction of hundreds of Japanese aircraft, submarines, ships, and barges.

Navy Admiral Halsey, who said that the intelligence signaled from Bougainville by Australians Paul Mason and Jack Read saved Guadalcanal, and that Guadalcanal The success of the Coastwatchers was praised by many, including U.S. saved the Pacific. High praise indeed.

intelligence information on Japanese troop, aircraft, and shipping movements while staying out of enemy hands. Rescuing downed airmen was important—but secondary to their main job.

The other white members of Captain Skinner's team were John Skokie, a former plantation manager, and Sergeant Matt Foley, a signals specialist. Stokie had arranged an earlier rescue of a B-26 bomber crew shot down outside Rabaul. When I asked again about my chances of being rescued, Skinner smiled ruefully and promised to send a signal back to headquarters. Then he added apologetically that any immediate attempt to evacuate me would jeopardize his party.

I understood his position, but told him I had been an amateur radio operator in peacetime and would be glad to lend a hand with the radio transmitter. Matt Foley was the only signal man in the party, so he was pleased with this information. As a matter of fact, he thought it might be a good idea to set up a second outpost right there near the beach. I could stay and relay information about enemy barge traffic. It all sounded good to me. I was anxious to be involved with something constructive. The next day Skinner headed back to his camp in the hills to get the portable radio set and some provisions. Since I was still too ill to travel fast, he decided that I should remain at the village on the beach. Before leaving he gave me some extra ammunition and a medicine kit with a good supply of quinine to suppress my malaria.

On the day Skinner was scheduled to return, Gabu, two other natives, and I paddled up the river a short way to meet him. The afternoon faded away with no sign of him. I began to fear that a Japanese patrol had overtaken his party. Then I remembered the extreme caution that Skinner had told me he used in the jungle. He always sent one native ahead of the main body of his party. The native carried a spear and pretended to be hunting pigs. If he met anyone suspicious, he would shout something in his native tongue that the enemy couldn't understand, thus signaling the danger to Skinner and his party in the rear.

Just when we had given up hope of seeing Skinner that night and were about to turn around and go back, we heard a strange whistle. A native man appeared on the trail. He told us that the others were close behind, bringing some cargo, and that Skinner had stayed back. Then he gave me a note from Skinner saying that he could join me as soon as he and his comrades received their supplies. It was pitch dark when the rest of the carriers arrived. They loaded the cargo into our canoe and we made the trip back to the beach without incident. We quickly unloaded the cargo and stowed it in the luluai's hut. In one of the parcels I found a new uniform, some woolen socks, and a much-needed pair of shoes. The size-forty pants were large enough to hold me and another whole person. I put them on and cinched up my belt, giving the carriers a good laugh. The food boxes contained condensed milk, cheese, honey, corned beef, tomato juice, sandwich spread, and a tin of plum pudding. We also found cigarettes, plenty of soap and shaving equipment, and a kerosene storm lamp. I went to sleep that night feeling as though Santa had stopped by.

Early the next morning we moved the cargo to a hut on the edge of a bluff overlooking the river. This new location could only be reached by wading through the water, so there were no trails to give our hideout away. The jungle around the hut was thick enough to swallow a man ten paces away. In a few minutes the natives had built another lean-to that served as a cookhouse and living quarters for the native guards.

The first meal in my new home was quite a contrast to the diet of snails I had enjoyed so long before. Gabu danced with joy when he saw all the different things he had to work with. But evidently he had learned to cook from the Australians, who use curry powder the way Americans use catsup. His stew of wild pig meat and dehydrated vegetables was excellent—except for an overdose of curry. It was some time before I could convince him that *Masta bilong America* did not like such spicy dishes.

After lunch I went to the creek, found a quiet pool, and sat down to give myself a scrubbing with actual soap—my first real bath in five months! When I finished digging the dirt out of my pores, my body seemed pounds lighter. And with a soapy lather and sharp razor I removed the hirsute evidence of my lack of grooming tools. When I was dressed in the clothes Skinner had sent, baggy as they were, I strutted proudly down to the village for native inspection. I felt as jaunty as an ad in Esquire.

One morning Quali brought news that all villagers without exception were to assemble at a place called Buteolo to meet *namba-wan bilong Japan.* Evidently the Japanese were worried about the natives giving information to the allied forces in the event of an invasion. Luluai Lauo was afraid they would torture him into informing on the presence of the Coastwatchers. He sent Gabu to the meeting with a message that he couldn't come himself because of bad foot sores. Gabu returned a few days later saying that the luluai's absence had made the Japanese suspicious and so they were sending a patrol to the village to investigate. I scribbled a message to Skinner, informing him of the situation, and dispatched a runner up to his camp.

Four days later Skinner arrived with a party of natives carrying several boxes of supplies that had been dropped from a supply plane the night before. One of them was from my own squadron. I rushed to open it and discovered another uniform (this time only three times too large), a pair of GI shoes, two bottles of brandy (an attached note said quite plainly that it was for medicinal purposes only), a thirty-caliber carbine still covered with packing grease, and an unabridged copy of Bocaccio's *Decameron*.

After unpacking my own things, I helped Skinner get the portable radio set out of its box and operating. I had been listening for only about five minutes when a message from headquarters in Port Moresby came through. Skinner appeared very nervous and excited as he decoded the message. When he passed it over to me, I learned that Moresby intelligence had word that enemy patrols were searching for us. The message further warned us to pack up and move inland immediately.

After a brief conference with Luluai Lauo, we decided to transfer all of the equipment to a spot back in the swamps. Loading a canoe as rapidly as possible, we headed for the marshland on the Pandi River. We later learned that a Japanese patrol had entered the village less than an hour after we had departed. By that time we were safely hidden in the thickest, most impenetrable jungle I'd ever seen. Huge sago palm roots stuck out of the water like octopus tentacles. When our canoe passed close to shore, vines and branches swiped our faces, covering us with cobwebs. Occasionally a crocodile would glide off of its resting place on the bank and come to investigate. The mosquitoes hung over and around us like a heavy cloud of smoke.

About midnight the paddlers guided the canoe up to a steep bank and unloaded the equipment. While some of the natives climbed tall trees to watch for patrols, the rest of us set up the portable radio and called headquarters in Port Moresby. Upon learning of our position, they ordered us to move further inland and again urged us to be extremely cautious. Our watching station, if successful, would provide valuable information for an impending allied operation.

Early the next morning we broke camp and traveled several hours by canoe to a spot where the rapids made further water travel impossible. We would have to go the rest of the way on foot. The native carriers set a fast pace. I had slipped on a single-log bridge and wrenched my knee, so it was impossible for me to keep up. I trailed along behind as best I could, falling down on the slippery trail a thousand times and trying to forget the sharp pain in my leg. Once, when crossing a swollen river, we had to cut poles and fashion a long handrail to keep from being swept downstream in the waist-deep current. Many times the trail led through patches of tall kunai grass with razor-sharp edges. As we walked atop the narrow ridges, the hot rays of the sun turned the jungle into a devil's steam bath.

When we reached our destination late that afternoon, I was completely exhausted and numb from the pain in my leg. But I immediately felt better when a cluster of natives and two white men came down the trail to meet us. The white men introduced themselves at Lieutenant John Stokie and Corporal Matt Foley. By strange coincidence, Stokie turned out to be the writer of the note that Luluai Lauo was carrying when his tribe found me by the river. John explained that in peacetime he was the superintendent of a coconut plantation. He knew the natives and the country well, and had stayed behind when the Australians evacuated Rabaul at the beginning of the hostilities. He had rescued the surviving members of a B-26 crew and escaped with them from the island in a Catalina flying boat. Then he returned with Skinner and Foley to set up the aircraft spotting system.

The lookout station was located at one end of a high ridge overlooking the dense jungle valleys below. To the north lay the placid blue waters of Open Bay. A high-powered telescope mounted on a sturdy pole could detect any enemy ships en route from Rabaul to Cape Gloucester. Enemy airplanes on their way from Rabaul to raid allied bases in New Guinea had to pass almost directly over-head. At night we could see searchlights sweeping across the sky as our own bombers unloaded over Rabaul. Sometimes we heard a B-24 returning to Port Moresby, and we watched the tracers squirt out from its tail gun as Japanese night-fighters tried to intercept.

The main hut at the camp housed the wireless set and our living quarters. The roof, covered with bundles of kunai grass, rotted quickly under the daily rains and had to be re-covered with fresh grass almost constantly. Nearby, two bamboo-covered lean-tos served as the *haus waswas* (bathroom) and *haus kuk* (kitchen). A leaky bucket provided our showers, but because the water had to be carried from a spring half a mile away, we only allowed ourselves two per week.

After supper Matt showed me the wireless set and explained its operation. Messages could be sent in voice or code. A tiny gasoline generator supplied power to charge the batteries. That night when we tuned in on the short-wave frequencies, the sound of orchestra music from a nightclub ten thousand miles away in San Francisco gave me an eerie feeling, as though I were living in two worlds.

Matt and I were working at the radio the next morning when a line of unfamiliar natives coming up the trail raised an alarm in the camp. Captain Skinner went out to meet them. Luckily they turned out to be members of a friendly tribe who brought news of two Royal Australian Air Force men who were hiding with them on the south coast. Their plane had been shot down over Jacquinot Bay during a strafing run. The native spokesman said he didn't know how long the airmen would be safe. Knowing they were somewhere on the island, the Japanese were threatening to torture the natives unless they gave them up. Skinner packed a few things immediately and left early the next morning with two of his carriers and the visitors.

The next day we received a message from Moresby saying that a supply drop would be attempted that night, weather permitting. We sent some men out to gather dry wood for the signal fires and made other preliminary preparations. Shortly before midnight we followed a guide through the jungle to a nearby garden where the drop was to take place. We arranged three fires to form a triangle, with the apex pointing north, and then went back into the bush to wait.

At five minutes past midnight we heard the telltale drone of a twin-engine Catalina flying boat. I dumped a small tin of kerosene on one of the fires and quickly stepped back as the flames shot skyward. The sound of the plane broke into a roar as it flew overhead. Tiny blue flames leaped from the exhaust stacks and an Aldis lamp blinked a recognition signal. Using his flashlight, Matt answered in Morse code. The plane then made a wide, sweeping turn and headed back toward our signal fires. I thought it was dangerously low for such a lumbering old crate to be flying over hilly terrain.

While I was shaking my head at the cold-blooded nerve of the pilot, a box came hurtling out of one of the plane's side blisters. The darkness swallowed it up for a moment and then it reappeared, dangling from the shroud lines of a small parachute. One of the

62

natives let out a whoop and dashed toward the spot where he thought it would land.

The Catalina made three additional runs across the area. Thirteen more parachutes filled the sky. We located all but the two that were carried beyond the drop zone by a sudden gust of wind. It would be impossible to find them until morning. We quickly gathered the others while the natives worked feverishly to destroy any evidence of the operation. By sunrise any enemy patrol that wandered into the clearing would find nothing but an elderly native working his garden.

We spent most of the next morning unpacking the boxes. One of them, sent by my squadron-mates, contained a camera, a case of beans, a bottle of gin, and some personal mail. I was flabbergasted to find myself reading a letter from my mother two hundred miles behind enemy lines. She said the war department had informed her that I was back under military control. She didn't know exactly what that meant, but assumed I was alive and no longer missing in action. Knowing that she now knew I was alive lifted my spirits. With four sons serving in the armed forces, I knew my parents were carrying a monstrous load of concern for our safety.

I also found a letter from *Time* imploring me to take advantage of a special new magazine subscription rate for service personnel. It seems my subscription had expired, and if I would just slip the enclosed card into the nearest mailbox, they would take care of the rest. (Of course, about the only value their offer had out there in the jungle was as fire-starting material.)

The next morning the roar of approaching planes interrupted our breakfast. We identified them as Japanese dive-bombers, about eighty in all. We estimated their speed and course, and flashed the news to headquarters. Two hours later we heard them returning. It was a wonderful sight. They appeared singly, in pairs, and in no formation at all, most of them limping along like wounded ducks. One straggler suddenly dropped its nose, plummeted out of control, and crashed in flames on the other side of the valley. Altogether we could account for fewer than twenty of the original eighty planes. Evidently our early warning flash had given our fighters just the break they needed to score a big win.

A few days later, on Christmas Day 1943, Skinner appeared in camp with the two RAAF airmen from the south coast—Wing Commander Bill Townsend and his gunner Dave McClymont. They had been on a raid at Pal Mal Mal in their Boston A-20 attack bomber when some lucky ack-ack shells knocked out their fuel system. Townsend ditched the plane in the water a few miles down the coast from a Japanese outpost, where they managed to get to shore in a rubber dinghy just a few minutes before an enemy patrol arrived on the beach. After wandering in the jungle for ten days, they were found by friendly natives, who hid them until they could get word to Captain Skinner.

That same day the radio brought news that our forces had landed on Cape Gloucester on the western tip of New Britain. A short time later a huge flight of Japanese dive-bombers escorted by about forty Zeros passed overhead in the direction of the cape. We radioed a report to headquarters, and to the American fighter control center. We could actually hear their loudspeakers warn our P-38 pilots of the impending raid. Tuning in to the fighter frequencies, we heard the jubilant shouts of the pilots as they spotted the enemy targets. We kept track of their progress by marking up the score each time one of our P-38's knocked a Japanese plane out of the sky.

Several days later we got word that another Japanese patrol was out searching for us. One of the natives told us that three workboats carrying enemy troops had landed at Ulamona Mission about eight miles from our station. It would be only a matter of days before the patrol would stumble onto our campsite. The two Aussies and I started out with a couple of native guides and some supplies to find a new and safer hideout. Captain Skinner and his team remained behind and planned to send runners to us with messages about the proximity of the Japanese patrol. We set out with a heavy rain beating down on our backs, and although it made traveling difficult, we were consoled by the knowledge that it would wash away our tracks and slow up any enemy patrols that might be in the vicinity.

We spent the first night shivering under the leaky roof of a makeshift lean-to. The wood was too wet to burn, and even if we had managed a fire, the smoke would have given away our position. Discretion dictated that we endure the best we could.

The next morning the rain had stopped. We found the jungle so impenetrable that we often had to crawl on our hands and knees. After sliding down a two-hundred-foot drop, we discovered a perfect place to pitch camp. Using hand grenades, we set out some booby traps and stationed guards around the perimeter. Finally we felt secure and lay down for our first good sleep in several days.

A full week went by before we got our first message from Skinner. The Japanese patrol had reached a spot about a mile below him—but they were afraid to cross the rain-swollen river and so had finally turned back to the beach. The good news was short-lived, however. A runner from our main camp brought word that a coast-watching station near Gasmata on the south coast had been captured by the Japanese because a native-turned-traitor had led an enemy patrol to the hideout. Was there a Judas in our party also? We couldn't let suspicion color our attitude; we had to depend on the natives for our survival in the jungle.

It took us three days to find our way back to the main camp. When we finally arrived I was exhausted. Another bout of malaria and a siege of dysentery had drained my last ounce of energy. Our first-aid kit yielded some sulfaquinedine pills but no instructions for its use. We radioed headquarters and were told that the first dose was fourteen pills. I stared at the huge things—they looked big enough to choke a horse. It just didn't seem possible. A second query brought the same answer: "Yes, fourteen pills." I swallowed them down.

One morning after I had partially recovered, we heard the Milne Bay station calling us. A twenty-three-word message came whistling over the loudspeaker in dits and dahs. I took it for Stokie to decode. Slowly the letters turned into words. AIRMEN CAN BE EVACUATED.... I didn't wait to hear the rest. I walked to the door of the hut and stared into space. I could almost taste my mother's home cooking. It was an overwhelming sensation.

A few minutes later Stokie came out with the complete message: AIRMEN CAN BE EVACUATED IF THEY CAN REACH MOUTH OF KORININDI RIVER BY FOUR FEBRUARY. OTHERWISE, REMAIN AT PRESENT BASE. GOOD LUCK. This was the 30th of January. Five days to freedom.

We got out some maps and searched for the Korinindi River, but it was nowhere to be found. The natives had never heard of it either. We radioed headquarters to get the latitude and longitude for the pick-up. The reply came back: FOUR DEGREES FIFTY MINUTES SOUTH. ONE FIVE ONE DEGREES FORTY MINUTES EAST. We grabbed the map and I ran my finger along the coordinates. It stopped in the middle of the ocean.

Matt tapped out another query to Moresby. They said that our map was out of date, and that they would attempt to drop off a replacement in the morning, weather permitting. Frustration overcame whatever optimism we had felt. When had our map been *in* date? That night we got down on our knees and begged the Lord to bless us with fair weather.

Early the next morning we scrambled down to the drop site. Our prayers had been answered: the sun rose out of a clear blue sky. We heard the distant sound of an approaching plane, but it was coming from the direction of Rabaul. Could it be an enemy reconnaissance plane on patrol? Should we put out the signal fires? Or let them blaze away while we prayed?

The steady cadence of clearly synchronized engines echoed across the hills, coming closer and closer and finally rising to a staccato roar as the plane came out of the rising sun with a rush. It hung for an instant, silhouetted against the sky. Townsend smiled. He knew the sound. He had recognized the high single tail, the twin engines, and the short wingspread. It was a Boston A-20, probably from his own squadron.

We heard the pilot throttle back the engines as the ship dipped to make a low approach across our signal fires. A white parachute burst open above the clearing and a native rushed out to grab a black cylinder as it hit the ground. Inside was the latest edition of the Gazelle Peninsula chart. We located our campsite and Stokie ran his finger out from the grid coordinates. There it was in capital letters, underlined in red: KORININDI RIVER. As the crow flies it was only thirteen miles northeast of our camp, but by foot it was probably three times that far. Could we make it in the four days we had left?

I thought we should start at once, but Townsend, the senior officer of our party, wasn't sure that was such a good idea. If we didn't make it in time, we'd wind up on the beach without enough food for the long trip back. And what about the danger of being caught by a Japanese patrol?

"What the hell," I said. "I've waited nine months for this day. If we don't make it, at least we'll have an interesting walk."

McClymont echoed my feelings and Townsend finally gave in. Stokie went into a huddle with the natives. After some bickering about fees, he persuaded them to lead us to the Korinindi. There were no trails, so we would have to rely entirely on their jungle expertise. We filled our pockets with extra bullets and chocolate bars. Stokie and Matt, who were staying behind to operate the watch station, gave us letters to mail from Australia.

I regretted not being able to say goodbye to Captain Skinner. He had not yet returned from his investigation of Lake Hargy as a possible rescue site for a flying boat. (I later learned how Lake Hargy got its name. A topographic unit in Melbourne was developing maps from aerial photos taken by my squadron. Bill

Fairbank told the mapmaker that this newly discovered body of water was where I had gone down, and that I was probably shacked up there with a chocolate-colored blonde.)

We said our farewells and followed our guides down the trail. At noon we paused by a spring at the bottom of a deep ravine to fill our water bottles and get some much-needed rest. The other side of the ravine was a hazardous climb. Reaching the top much later, we looked back and realized it had taken four hours to travel only a stone's throw toward our ultimate destination. Discouragement set in and we began to wonder if we could possibly make it in four days.

The trail led along a ridge for a mile or so and then branched off in two directions. A light rain was falling. Our guide seemed confused about which way to go. Anxious to be on our way, we took one of the branches on a guess. Sixty minutes later we were back at the fork. Another hour wasted! We took the other branch and just before dark stumbled onto an inhabited clearing. Our guide coaxed a native out of his hut and persuaded him to let us spend the night there, sheltered from the rain.

While sitting around the fire in our host's guesthouse, we heard the sound of running steps and a loud commotion outside. I reached for my carbine and took off the safety. "Japanese?" McClymont whispered.

A dog sniffed at the edge of the door. We held our breaths as the sound of voices and footsteps came nearer. Then a single voice called out, "*Masta Predi.*"

"Hey Mac," I yelled. "It's Lauo, the luluai from Ae Ae."

We fell all over ourselves scrambling out of the hut. There was my old friend with several others from his village. They had brought food from the beach up to John Stokie and learned that we were on our way to be rescued. They wanted to say goodbye. I explained to Lauo that our evacuation would probably have to be postponed because of the heavy rains. He conferred with our guide and then said he was confident that a way could be found to get us there in time.

Before sunrise the next morning we set off with a new guide in the pouring rain. First we went south, skirting a ravine, then northeast up a hill and down muddy tracks. After lunch we came to a barrier that effectively stopped our trek in that direction. It was a stream, a torrent of brown foaming water impossible to cross. So we turned back, and eventually came upon two deserted houses where we decided to camp for the night. The next morning, after three hours of walking, we arrived at the village we had left the morning before! We were disheartened to say the least. After two and a half days we were only a half-day's walk from our starting point. Then in came some natives, sent by John Stokie to tell us that we needed to proceed as quickly as possible because the pick-up time had been moved forward.

The following morning we set off with a hill native guide and plenty of carriers. We struggled forward at a relentless pace. Finally the rain stopped, which allowed us to cross the stream that had held us up the previous day. Soon we came to another one that was still muddy and flowing strongly. Undaunted, our carriers built a temporary bridge out of logs lashed together with vines. We made a successful crossing, and then about mid-afternoon we reached the second-largest swamp in New Britain. Following a slow-moving river and occasionally fording small tributaries, we came upon a huge tree that had fallen across the water. Once on the other side, we slogged through a rotting, stinking sago-palm swamp. That night we slept in a hastily erected shelter beside a crocodile-infested backwater. The next morning we started out early and made our way through the swamp alongside the sluggish Pandi River, sometimes up to our knees in mud and slime.

At eleven-thirty we reached the coast and took off our boots to avoid leaving tracks. We walked about a mile down the Japanese road to the spot where canoes were waiting to take us to the coastal village of Baia. A husky native policeman, sent by the other coast-watching station to guide us on the last leg, greeted us. The last leg? Hadn't we just completed the last leg of our trek? Then I discovered that the pick-up spot was across the bay, a two-day journey by foot. By that time our rescuers would have given us up and moved on, so I knew our only hope was to paddle across the bay in a canoe. None of the natives wanted to risk taking us in daylight however—too many Japanese patrol boats. I pulled out some razor blades and a knife to barter. We made a deal. A few minutes later we climbed into a canoe with two strong natives.

We were halfway across when one of the men spotted a sail in the distance. Was it a Japanese patrol boat? We made some emergency plans. Townsend, McClymont, and I would lie in the bottom of the canoe with our carbines at ready. If the patrol boat hailed us, we would come alongside and at a given signal pop out from under the camouflage and spray the enemy with our guns. But luck was with us! For some strange reason the patrol boat never bothered us. We reached the other shore with nothing damaged but our nerves.

We paid off the native paddlers and sent them back across the bay. The sun disappeared as we followed the policeman along the shore. We began to speculate how we would be rescued, and decided we would probably be picked up by a Catalina flying boat around midnight. We were taking our time along the beach when suddenly our guide pointed to a large black object resting in the water a few hundred yards offshore.

"An island," I said.

"*No, no, Masta*," he whispered, "*em i gumi bot.*"

"Em i what?" I asked, still seeing little cause for excitement. But Townsend grabbed my arm excitedly and I knew then what an *i gumi bot* was.

"It's a submarine," Townsend whispered incredulously.

I looked again. There, rising and falling with the ocean swell, was a large sub with its conning tower silhouetted against the sky. We didn't dare shout, but we ran on as fast as we could. Suddenly about six natives armed with guns jumped out of the mangroves. They were the rear guard, put there to cover our departure. We spotted two rubber boats a couple hundred yards offshore and headed for the submarine. Just then an Australian commando stepped out of the darkness and signaled with his flashlight that three more aviators had arrived. The next few minutes felt like an eternity. Had they given up on us? No. One of the boats finally turned around and headed back to shore. We raced out through the breakers and scrambled aboard. In a few minutes we were alongside the *USS Gato* with friendly hands helping us onto the deck. They rushed us to the conning tower and down into the bowels of this huge fish.

The skipper, Lieutenant Commander Bob Foley, greeted us and ordered the Six-B treatment: Bath, Bandage, Bread, Butter, Bouillon, and Bed.

I could have added another B. We had already been Blessed.

The Hargesheimer family, 1933.

Mary Louise Hargesheimer's first solo flight.

Fred in 1941 with his basic-training plane, the BT-13.

Pilots Hargesheimer, Guerry, and Hazzard prepare to join the 8th Photo Squadron.

Japanese pilot Mitsugu Hyakutomi. (If he hadn't shot Fred down over West New Britain in 1943, the Airmen's Memorial Schools would not exist!)

Wing Commander Bill Townsend, RAAF, and Fred prepare to leave the Coastwatcher campsite to avoid discovery by the Japanese.

Walter—with U.S. Marines
during invasion of Iwo Jima.

Richard—with U.S. Navy
Seabees in South Pacific.

Fred—pilot, U.S. Army Air
Corps.

Robert—flight engineer,
U.S. Army Air Corps.

The four Hargesheimer brothers.

Fred and Dorothy's wedding
day, December 16, 1944.

Fred and Dorothy with Carol, Dick, and Eric, 1959.

Luluai Lauo, 1960.

Fred with Robert and Ida Tagogo, 1960.

Nantabu villagers bid farewell to Fred in 1960.

Joseph Gabu, 1963.

Dick and friends, 1963.

Fred and Dorothy in Ewasse, 1971.

Dorothy presents Garua Peni with her sixth-grade diploma in 1971.

Dorothy and students in Rabaul, 1974.

Saura Auru Fred Hargesheimer, 2000.

Fred with friends at Hennessey School.

HOME AT LAST

After disembarking at Dreger Harbor, we went by jeep to the airstrip at Finschhafen, where we boarded a C-47 for the trip to Brisbane. The intelligence officer at Headquarters of the Allied Air Forces, Southwest Pacific Area, wrote up EE (Enemy Evader) Report No. 34 covering my experience in New Britain. The Coastwatchers was a super-secret organization; I would not be allowed to speak about my experiences to anybody except air force personnel with a secret clearance and a "need to know."

At this time I learned that I had been promoted to captain while behind enemy lines. Another happy surprise came when I visited the paymaster at the Lennon's Hotel in Brisbane: a nice check for nine months' worth of back pay. It did not cover meals and lodging while on temporary duty, but it did include the usual fifty percent extra for flight pay—even though I hadn't done any flying.

I asked General Kenney if I could go back to the squadron, but he said I owed it to my family to see them before deciding my future. So a week later I climbed aboard a C-24 air transport for the trip back to the States.

My first stop was the air force headquarters at the Pentagon for another debriefing. Did I have any suggestions for jungle survival? What was it like to bail out of a P-38? Orders granting me a ten-day leave and a plane ticket home to Rochester, Minnesota gave me a chance to visit my family and friends. It was hard to refrain from sharing the details of my experience. I needed to talk, to unload what I had been carrying around for so many months. But I had been sworn to secrecy, so that would have to wait until after the hostilities had ended. I learned that two of my brothers, Walt and Richard, were somewhere in the South Pacific with the marines and the Seabees, respectively.

After ten days of stuffing myself with home cooking, I flew off to California for two weeks of R&R at the Miramar Hotel on the beach at Santa Monica. A reunion with my beloved Aunt Floss, a tour of the Fox Film Studio, and lunch at the Paramount Studio with Linda Darnell were the highlights of my visit.

At air force headquarters back in Washington, DC, I was temporarily assigned to the reconnaissance branch of the Office of Commitments and Requirements to work with Rummy Foster, a former squadron-mate. My primary duty was to race around the corridors of the Pentagon coordinating overseas cables generated by the reconnaissance branch. This usually entailed getting signatures from five different departments. Each time any one of them changed as much as a single word—whether or not it changed the intent of the message—I had to get everyone's approval all over again. Being a messenger boy was not to my liking, so I put in for a transfer to the third reconnaissance wing located at Smoky Hill Air Force Base near Salina, Kansas. The commander, Colonel Pat MacCarthy, was assembling a squadron of B-29 bombers stripped of all armaments and outfitted with the latest aerial cameras. Our destination was the tiny island of Saipan in the Central Pacific, where our mission was to photograph all of Japan and develop maps for use by the B-29s that would follow us to Saipan and Tinian islands.

I never got to experience the thrill of flying the air force's biggest bomber. Shortly after my arrival I was called into the commander's office. He had seen the reference to malaria on my medical record and wanted no part of Captain Hargesheimer. He thought malaria was contagious and was afraid I would infect the whole squadron. The next morning I was on a courier flight back to Washington, DC.

The commanding officer's ignorance about malaria turned out to be a blessing for me. Had I stayed with the squadron and gone back overseas, I probably never would have met the lovely girl who later became my wife and the mother of our three wonderful children.

She was Dorothy Sheldon of Ashtabula, Ohio. We were never formally introduced. Our first meeting was over the Eastern Airlines counter at Washington National Airport. She was the attractive agent checking in passengers for a flight to Alabama. I was bound for Birmingham on official business for the U.S. Air Force. The fact that my shiny new captain's bars did not impress her was a serious blow to my ego. I tried to get her telephone number for my little black book—but no luck. I was determined to remedy the situation as soon as I returned from my trip.

Persistence has its rewards. After numerous refusals, Dorothy finally accepted an invitation to go out with me. We soon discovered that we had compatible chemistries. A trip to Ashtabula introduced me to her delightful family. After a grilling by her Uncle Bob, my intentions were considered honorable.

I had not planned to formalize our relationship with a diamond ring, but Dorothy's sister Carol encouraged me to reconsider or risk dire consequences. On my next trip to California I shared my dilemma with Aunt Floss. Her boss Harry Sherman, producer of the *Hop Along Cassidy* films, had lots of connections in Hollywood. One of his friends was in the jewelry business, so I was able to buy a diamond ring at wholesale. I think Dorothy always secretly admired me for my pragmatism.

Anyway, the ring sealed our love affair. Four months later, on December 16, 1944, the Reverend John Hudley united us in holy matrimony—as witnessed by best man Colonel John G. Foster and maid of honor Priscilla Sherman. The wedding in Ashtabula, Ohio, was a memorable affair. I flew out to Cleveland from Washington via commercial airline two days early. Colonel Foster and Harlan Olson, an 8th Photo squadron-mate, followed the next afternoon in an AT-6 training plane. That same morning a winter storm blew in across Lake Erie, dumping a record snowfall on the Cleveland Airport. When Foster and Olson finally landed, the snow was so deep that their plane got stuck on the taxiway and had to be towed by a tractor to the parking ramp. Later they told me that landing on instruments in the blinding snow was not nearly as frightening as their wild ride with Uncle Bob, who had driven them from Cleveland to Ashtabula.

A reception at the Ashtabula Hotel followed the ceremony at the Congregational Church. Then, shortly after we cut the cake, a sudden attack of malaria cut the evening short. Our wedding suite was converted into a hospital room, and there I was, the shivering groom (now about as romantic as a flat tire), put to bed to suffer through the malady. Between shakes and sweats I asked myself, "Who said life was fair?" But my bride's tender ministrations were most welcome.

I did manage to recover in time for us to catch the morning train to Buffalo with connections to Montreal and a honeymoon in the snowy mountains of Canada. I had arranged some private ski lessons for Dorothy, but when she stuck her nose into the subzero air outside, she decided that a book by the fireside was more to her liking. Since I had already paid for the lessons, I had no choice but to stand in for her. The instructor turned out to be an instructress—a charming young lady with a French accent, a detail I conveniently overlooked when I reported back to Dorothy.

The next day I got a telegram from Colonel McCoy, my boss at the Pentagon. "Since you are no longer a minor, proceed at once to earn the extra ration allowance offered to a higher-grade officer's family." It was his way of telling me that I had been promoted to major and as such would be entitled to three ration allowances if we had a child.

When we returned to Washington, I was greeted with War Department Special Orders No. 301, dated 16 December 1944, promoting me to major. My monthly base pay was $236, plus flight pay of $118, plus the extra subsistence allowance of $44.10 and a rental allowance of $90, making a grand total of $488.10.

Dorothy and I set up housekeeping in a one-bedroom apartment at Lee Gardens across the highway from the west gate of Fort Meyers. Our furniture included a double bed, a card table, a secondhand sofa from my parents in Minnesota, a lounge chair, and a six-foot Steinway grand piano. My raise qualified us to buy some bedroom furniture on an installment plan, and Dorothy's 1939 Chevy coupe provided us with transport.

We discovered that Dorothy was pregnant. That was a momentous development—and cause for joy mixed with a bit of trepidation. The extra subsistence allowance was very welcome. Our apartment had no air-conditioning, and a hot and humid Washington summer is a miserable time for a mother-to-be. Many nights we spread a blanket on the lawn and joined the rest of the residents sleeping under the stars.

The day the bells at Westminster in London signaled the end of the war in Europe was the day our first child began to kick up his heels. He wanted out. A few weeks later, on August 16, 1945, Dick was born at the base hospital at Bulling Field across the Potomac from the Pentagon. Forty-eight hours after the delivery Dorothy was sent home. And in spite of bouts of colic, hours walking the floor, and the various other difficulties we faced while rearing Dick through infancy, he was our bargain baby. Total birthing cost at the hospital was forty dollars.

It was decision-making time for us. Should I stay in the military—or opt out and look for a civilian job? The first option had an attractive incentive: the air force offered me a chance to apply for an advanced degree at one of many leading colleges. It was tempting. I could sign on for another four years and earn a master's degree in electrical engineering—all at government expense. The only hitch was that I would be assigned to an officers' pool in Dayton, Ohio—and would have to wait for an opening at one of the universities. Dorothy said she would do whatever I thought best. Because of the uncertainty about how long we would have to stay in Dayton, and the fact that a playmate for Dick was already on the way, I chose, with Dorothy's approval, to look for a civilian job.

When my former boss Major Armstrong offered me an engineering position at his FM research station in Alpine, New Jersey, I gladly accepted. And then on November 12, 1946, our number-two son Eric joined the family. Right before he was born the nurse insisted that Dorothy wasn't ready to deliver, but Dorothy knew better! He was quiet and calm—perfect qualities for a second child.

My new job had a special perk: during the summer, I managed a field test site at West Hampton, Long Island. Armstrong rented a splendacious beach house called Sandringham, where we erected antennas to study the propagation characteristics of FM broadcasts from the laboratory at Alpine. Charlie Chaplin had been the previous year's tenant; Lena Horne was our neighbor to the east. Five bedrooms and the same number of bathrooms provided ample accommodations for our family. (The two boys delighted in trying out each one. We finally put an end to this practice by closing three of the bathroom doors with ten-penny nails.) I used one of the bedrooms as an office where I kept the field-strength recording instruments.

Carol came along on December 29, 1947, during one of the heaviest snowstorms in New York City's history. Thanks to the helping hands of our neighbors, who shoveled out a path on our one-block-long street, I was able to get our car out to the main road. I had my first glimpse of Carol when the nurse brought her to the waiting room. She was a beautiful child. I marveled at her newborn perfection—and had to grin at the sight of a tiny green ribbon someone had tied in her hair.

I HAD TO GO BACK

In 1951 Bill Butler, an old Iowa Stage College classmate, was instrumental in getting me a job with the Sperry Rand Corporation's ERA (Engineering Research Associates) Division, which later became the UNIVAC (Universal Automatic Computer) Division. (Their UNIVAC 1 was the very first commercial digital computer on the market.) We sold our house in Englewood, New Jersey, and moved to White Bear Lake, Minnesota.

When I arrived at the ERA plant on West Minnehaha Avenue in St. Paul, I knew absolutely nothing about digital computers, so I spent the first six weeks attending in-house computer classes. In the meantime, ERA was awarded a government contract to design an antenna coupler for airborne use. Because of my previous experience with radio frequency equipment, I was asked to work on this new project. Shortly after we completed the first prototype model, ERA received a contract from the Boeing Airplane Company to develop a similar device for their 707 commercial jet. Since our computer sales personnel knew nothing about radio equipment, I was given responsibility for marketing the antenna coupler. The program enjoyed a profitable success for many years.

During the cold Minnesota winters my thoughts often returned to my friends on that warm island in the South Pacific. Something kept reaching out to me from the village of Ae Ae—now called Nantabu—on the island of New Britain. It was the obligation I felt to the people who had saved my life. After my plane was shot down over the tropical wilderness, they had hidden me many times at great danger to themselves. They had also nursed me through several life-threatening illnesses. I wondered how I could ever thank Ida Tagogo, whose mother's milk was the only food my desperately ill body would accept.

Finally, in 1960, I decided I had to go back and express my gratitude. But when a war is over and a man is no longer a warrior, his obligation is to his family. Airplane tickets were expensive and our savings account thin. But Dorothy said she understood. The three kids, of course, were growing up with the oft-told tales of my South Seas adventures, and they too understood my need to return. They agreed to forego our vacation that year and let me set off to re-unite with my friends in that tiny South Pacific backwater

By then our boys were actually young men who said goodbye with handshakes, a milestone. I gave our daughter Carol a fatherly hug—and my wife a mighty embrace.

My compulsion to go back overrode any concerns about possible danger. All of us seemed to feel that this was as necessary as going to church on Sunday. But would Luluai Lauo still be there? Gabu? Ida? The maps of that area now showed Lake Hargy, permanent proof of what the military had endured there. Had the intervening sixteen years dimmed the memory of the man they called "*Masta Predi*"? This could turn out to be an expensive, frustrating junket.

The trip required preparation, so I went through the business of vaccination shots, paid eighteen hundred dollars for plane tickets, and acquired my travel documents. The night before I left, I dreamed uneasily of getting lost in the jungle, of not finding the village, and—most disturbing of all—of not finding anyone I knew.

In San Francisco I boarded a Qantas 707 jet. An overnight stop in Honolulu revealed nothing but an endless series of hotels with a palm tree squeezed in here and there. The next day our plane was headed for Sydney, Australia. The crew invited me to the flight deck, and from there I saw the pink glow that heralded the rising sun, spectacular at any time but breathtaking when viewed from above. Puffy clouds beneath the plane were like balls of cotton bobbing above the water. I hadn't enjoyed that phenomenon since flying my unarmed P-38 photo-reconnaissance plane over New Britain during the war.

A group of reporters, photographers, and TV newsmen crowded around me when I got off the plane at Kingsford-Smith Airport in Sydney. I was completely flabbergasted. It turned out they had been waiting for the arrival of U.S. Navy Admiral Hopwood, who was scheduled to take part in a memorial for the men who had participated in the Battle of the Coral Sea (an important turning point in Japan's efforts to capture New Guinea and thus directly threaten Australia). He was late so the newsmen descended on me. The next day's stories had one good effect: my hotel phone kept ringing and once again I heard the voices of old squadron-mates and other friends from those war years.

There was Air Vice-Marshall Bill Townsend, the Australian who had also been shot down by the Japanese. He was later rescued by the same American submarine, the *USS Gato*, that took us off the island after over eight months in the jungle. Then Ralph Bray, formerly with the Australian forces, strolled in. He asked me to be sure to tell the man he remembered as Colonel Charlie Mayo how grateful he was. (Bray's hand had been seriously wounded while he was camped in the Markham Valley. When surgeons wanted to remove one of his fingers, the famous doctor from Minnesota advised against it.) Bray held up his hand and wiggled his fingers at me. They all worked.

It would have been easy to indulge in old-home week, but time was of the essence and I wanted to keep moving towards the jungle. So I left Sydney in a Lockheed Constellation headed for Port Moresby, New Guinea—now called Papua New Guinea. There were plenty of forms to fill out because New Britain was under a trusteeship, not part of Australia. I remember the question "What is your connubial condition?" I thought that was a strange way of asking whether or not I was married.

We stopped at Brisbane, Australia, and there was Ian Skinner, the first white man I had seen after all those months in hiding. I was so filled with emotion that merely shaking his hand seemed altogether too formal. When he told me that Luluai Lauo was still there, and that not only did the villagers remember me, but that word of my return was spreading through the jungle, the rest of the trip couldn't move fast enough.

The sun was barely over the horizon when we started our letdown over Port Moresby. We were fifteen minutes early, so the captain of the plane cruised around the area where my old squadron's airstrip had been. It was completely gone—the jungle had closed back in over it.

In the front of the airport waiting room stood Alan Roberts, one of the Coastwatchers rescued by the *USS Gato* and now the director of Papua New Guinea's Department of Native Affairs. It was hard to believe that all of us who struggled together for survival in the jungle seventeen years earlier were meeting here as if it had all been planned.

My gear was shifted to a Douglas DC-4 for the flight north to Lae. As we climbed up to clear the tips of the Owen Stanley Mountains, I recalled the many times I needed to put full power on my P-38 in order to get off our airstrip and scrape over those fourteen-thousand-foot peaks as I set out across the Bismarck Sea to New Britain.

When the plane door opened at Lae, the bake-oven heat of the tropics hit me. The remains of a sunken Japanese naval vessel lay rusting just off the end of the runway. I remembered how often I had made photo runs over that same Lae airstrip to get pictures for our operations people. The Japanese ack-ack guns could bracket a plane very well, so I had to take evasive maneuvers whenever the puffs of black smoke burst out near the tips of the wings. Of course the worst thing about it (or so I told myself at the time) was the fact that it messed up the pictures I was trying to take.

For the flight to Rabaul on the far end of New Britain, I switched planes again—this time to a DC-3. The Qantas ground crew was made up almost entirely of natives wearing laplaps, their traditional wraparound skirts. Soon we were flying over the jungle I had known so intimately. A foot, a minute, an hour, a day at a time I had learned to know it—the vegetation, the trees, the sounds or absence of sounds so different from home. Would I ever again be able to look at the jungle without having the loneliness of those thirty-one days rise up and envelope me?

We tried to fly over Lake Hargy and have a look, but the heavy clouds that always cover the jungle in late afternoon made it impossible to see. On landing at Rabaul I found another of my jungle buddies, Matt Foley, the radio operator for the Coastwatchers team. I had last seen him when I took leave of his communications campsite and hiked over to Open Bay to be picked up by the submarine. Anyone who hasn't experienced such reunions can't imagine a couple of grown men getting as emotional as we did.

The question at this point was how to get back to my jungle village of Nantabu. I needn't have been concerned; Matt had great news. A government trawler at Rabaul that was scheduled to take a surveyor down the coast could drop me off there. John Foldi, the district commissioner, had already cleared the red tape. More and more it seemed that at every step I was exactly where I was supposed to be, with the way made clear.

The trawler had seen better days. Its name—*Mangana*—was just barely visible on the old scow. What remained of the paint was a chipped and faded red. A potbellied wood-burning stove on the afterdeck was the only evidence that food could be prepared onboard. A master (captain), a native engineer, and a native helmsman were the crew. The old tub was going to Lolobau Island, below Nantabu; they hoped to recruit some new crewmembers there. To them I suppose this looked like a fancy ship. To me it looked like better than nothing!

We crawled out of Simpson Harbor and shifted our course around the peninsula that was dominated by Mount Matupi (the "daughter" of a family of volcanoes that stretches along the entire length of New Britain). At seven knots, this last leg of my journey back to the jungle was quite a contrast to the 707 flight that began my trip from San Francisco. We had no water on board, just beer with a sixteen-percent alcohol content. We also had medicines, mail, tins of food, and other supplies for the isolated plantation men.

For the next sixteen hours we moved carefully along the jungle coastline. As we slid through the St. Georges channel between Rabaul and New Ireland, I remembered sighting a Japanese convoy there and radioing my home base. Through a misunderstanding in the code message, our bombers were sent to another place. I sure got chewed out for that one. Later I received the Distinguished Flying Cross for being the first man to get pictures of enemy bases further inland.

At five in the afternoon we nudged into the anchorage at Pondo. Earthquakes had spilled parts of the hillsides down into the ocean, leaving gashes in the deep green landscape. We tied up at an old broken-down wharf. The place seemed uninhabited. We blew the ship's horn and twenty minutes later Frank Vivian, the plantation manager, came down. He was a bachelor in his forties with a red goatee and glasses. We visited his house on the hill overlooking the harbor. He lived alone with a hundred natives working the plantation; his big dining room table had just one place setting. I noticed a huge stack of paperback books, a radio communications set, and a butterfly collection. He told me he hoped to take a four-month round-the-world tour the following year. I would have liked to ask him more about his life, so different from the London where he was born, but our trawler had to move on. The next stop would bring me to Nantabu, the village I had grown to know so intimately and whose people had meant life itself to me.

As we came down the coast we saw the sun setting over the top of Mount Ulawan (the "father" volcano), while at the same time the moon was rising on the other side of the boat. I felt a kind of tension grow within me. With a clank and a rattle, our anchor dropped. Nantabu has no beach: the mangrove and sago palms come right to the edge of the water. There was no dock, no mooring, nothing. For a minute it seemed strangely quiet. Were the villagers really there? Then we heard voices, and in the moonlight I could distinguish a native canoe with three men in it. I waved and shouted as it came closer. It was too dark to identify any of them, but I could tell they were much too young to be my old friends.

"*Yu Masta Predi?*" asked the man in the bow. I reached out and his hand met mine. When we let go, the canoe turned around and streaked for the shore. It apparently had been sent out on reconnaissance.

Then the big boys came out. Their canoe was made from a huge log with outriggers on each side. A board platform stretched out over one of them. Two paddlers stood in the bow, and two more stood astern. On the makeshift deck I could see seven figures dressed in a sort of a uniform made from bits and pieces of clothing from *taim bepo long bikpela pait* (World War II). Several sported visored hats with little ribbons around the crowns. They stood straight as telephone poles as the canoe came alongside. Each one had a row of medals awarded by the Australian government for his service to the allied forces. Their white laplaps glowed in the moonlight. They wore no shoes for the occasion, which seemed altogether proper.

What struck me first was the fact that each man wore a tie, but then I remembered how much they like to wear them—the brighter the better. (Among my things on the boat was a big bundle of ties I had bought at a rummage sale at the Wilderness Episcopal Church in White Bear Lake.)

Next I remember the sounds of voices lifted in song drifting from the shore. The songs were taken from old hymns, with twists in the melodies. Then a ceremonial canoe came alongside. It held Lauo, the luluai. He solemnly extended his hand and asked me to step across to his canoe. I shook hands all around and the paddlers moved the craft towards shore.

The moon was so bright that it cast shadows through the coconut trees. As we neared the shore I could see the people of the village in their Sunday best—white laplaps for the men, white blouses for the women. When I stepped ashore they broke into "God Save the Queen."

I could tell they had been planning this ceremonial welcome for some time, and later learned that they had expected me four days earlier. They had been waiting by the water all this time. Now here we were together again. The strange formality of the welcome, all carried out in the soft moonlight, was beautiful to me. These are a solemn people—no forced smiles or empty grins—but their ceremonies are filled with meaning. My cheeks were wet with tears. When it was over, they lined up and I shook each hand one by one. The mothers lifted their infants for me to touch and I took their tiny hands. It went on and on, and finally I realized why there seemed to be no end to the line of greeters: they were going to the back of the line and then working their way forward for another handshake.

Luluai Lauo made a speech in Pidgin. "The man we knew as a downed flier and the man we saw in the moonlight are one and the same." It was true—I had come back. I was overwhelmed with emotion.

I told them we had *planti tumas toktok* (plenty to talk about), and that our boat would bring me back at *no tulait* (predawn) before heading on down to Lolobau Island. It seemed a shame that they had gotten all dressed up for this half-hour of re-acquaintance by moonlight, but I knew a good night's sleep would put me in better shape for catching up on the years that had passed since our last meeting. At that point it seemed prudent to go back to the trawler and savor the knowledge that my dream of returning had become a reality.

We all stood on the platform atop the outriggers of the canoe and solemnly moved out to the trawler. Once aboard, I settled in for the night. Then, just as I began to doze off, I heard the sound of an outboard motor. I knew it wasn't my friends from the village. We called out into the night but got no answer. We could hear the sputter of the motor as the boat skirted the shore. A spotlight flashed from it and then all was quiet.

In the morning the man with the outboard appeared again. We learned that he was Keith Manning, a plantation manager who was hunting crocodiles. Turns out that the Pandi River is one of the best crocodile-hunting streams in the area. Keith got twenty-two of them in a space of five nights. The skins bring a fancy price and are made into shoes, boots, handbags, and belts.

At five the next morning we signaled to the natives on shore. Out came the canoes once more, and once more I was greeted with "*Masta Predi.*" This time Matt Foley went ashore with me. We found the tribe lined up again for the same handshaking ceremony, so Matt and I ran down the line, looking into the faces of these strong yet gentle people.

Suddenly Luluai Lauo called out, "*Harim olgeta yupela.*" He was about to make a speech and was asking everybody to gather round. My Pidgin, which I thought would be rusty, came back fast. "The man we know as Master Predi has come back," the luluai continued. "I want to talk to everybody about the time the war was going on." Then he described my whole set of experiences, from getting shot down to being taken off by submarine. He talked steadily for a good ten minutes or so.

In response I explained how grateful I was, and why I had to come back and tell them so. Then I presented them with some new laplap fabrics from Rabaul, along with the neckties from our church at home. The fabric was appreciated but the ties made the biggest hit.

One by one villagers who had been part of my rescue and survival were solemnly introduced. I remembered them—Balia, Kwali, Gabuli, and Galia. They looked me straight in the eye. Each of them showed me his loyalty service medal, but it didn't take a decoration for me to know their devotion. Then Luluai Lauo handed me a shiny half-crown coin. I had given it to him as a souvenir, and for sixteen years he had kept it buried in a tin can. I offered to buy it back from him, but he said no. To him it was a symbol of all that had happened, a promise that I might one day return. I knew there must have been many times when its monetary value might have overcome its sentimental value. I was deeply moved by this tangible token of his regard for me.

I inquired about my dear friend Gabu and learned that he had waited three days for me before needing to return to the distant village where he now lived. I also found out that the native missionary who had brought me the Bible had been killed by the Japanese during the last months of the war.

Luluai Lauo's wife asked if I remembered the cakes she used to bake for me. I certainly did. They were made of shredded coconut and tapioca. She hadn't changed much at all, but some of the natives didn't look familiar. Then I discovered that they were ringers brought in from neighboring villages to boost up the size of the reception. The beach had become a sort of parking lot crowded with visiting canoes. Each craft was a hollowed-out log, fashioned with traditional skill.

Next on the agenda was the *singsing*, a traditional celebration featuring native songs intermixed with missionary hymns. Baskets of yams, taro roots, and *kaukau* (sweet potatoes) were brought in. I didn't want to turn down this welcoming feast, but my doctor in Minnesota had minced no words about my innards and just how little they could handle. Matt Foley explained my predicament to the tribe in fluent Pidgin. He told them that *beli bilong Masta Predi* was not in very good shape. They all expressed sympathy. "*O Masta Predi, mi sori tumas.*"

While the natives ate their traditional delicacies, Matt and I heated a tin of spaghetti and sliced a loaf of bread. We didn't have a can opener, but Lauo showed up with a captured Japanese knife, a spoon, a fork—*and* a can opener. When we had finished eating I asked Lauo and his *tultul* (second-in-command) about my aircraft. Ever since parting company with my plane, I had wondered if it had ever been found.

Oh yes, they assured me. They knew where it was. But how far away? Ask a Nakanai native that and you've got a problem. It might be one mile or a hundred—what mattered was the number of nights on the trail. I asked several times. *"Hamas pela nait i stop long wokabaut?"*

"Em i go, i go, i go, i go, longwe tumas," they would answer.

The trawler was due back to pick me up, so I had to give up seeing my plane again. But the natives assured me that it was untouched. We did have time to climb into the canoes, paddle down the coast for about an hour, and go back into the bush to see their gardens, the ones that had kept me going all those months they had hidden me from the enemy.

It wasn't long after I got back to Nantabu that the *Mangana* appeared. The next ship might not come by for a week or a couple of months, so I had no choice but to take it. I didn't know when, or even if, I would ever get back. Again the line formed and again there was the solemn handshaking. I knew this must be as big a deal for them as it was for me. Their faces remained expressionless but the warmth of their handclasps told me everything. As I headed out to the trawler on the outrigger canoe, the luluai and his people stood straight and unmoving—but, I know, not unmoved.

My dream had become reality. I had returned to Nantabu— but where was Ida? When our trawler pulled into the wharf at Rabaul the next day, Reverend Wesley Lutton, chairman of the Methodist overseas mission, greeted me with the news that Ida and her family had come across nineteen miles of open sea from the Duke of York Islands in a tiny sixteen-foot boat. The mission station had received word that a launch was being sent for her, but Ida got impatient, loaded her family into the little craft, and made the trip.

After dinner I went to the Lutton's home. It was on the beach overlooking the harbor and the rusted remains of a Japanese cargo vessel, a wartime casualty. Ida was sitting in a chair in the living room with six of her seven children gathered around her on the floor. (Apelis, her husband, had died some time before.) She spoke only Maututu, the local language, so Pastor Lutton served as our interpreter. She actually smiled a little when I shook her hand.

Then I met the children one by one. The last was Robert, the newborn she had been nursing when I first knew her. Now he was a husky sixteen-year-old: both of us had survived. He became very shy when told who I was.

Finally, with some coaxing, Ida and her family sang for me. It was a moving rendition of "Onward Christian Soldiers" with some of the notes changed. I realized then just how much their firmness in their faith had enabled them to hold out against the Japanese. Time and again the natives were told that I was a foreigner, that I represented a white man's religion. But Lauo's people never wavered. When I was with them, they never missed a Sunday service—unless the Japanese were right there in the village.

I went to the beach and watched Ida and her family leave with the two men who had come to help paddle that sixteen-foot canoe. They turned and looked back at me. They didn't wave or smile, but their gaze was steady and long. Soon the canoe was a vanishing shadow on the blue water.

I returned home to Minnesota on a series of airplanes, each larger and faster than the one before. Ten thousand miles seemed to compress into hours. I brought along some souvenirs for my family. One, presented to me by Luluai Lauo, was the conch shell they had used to warn me of approaching Japanese planes and patrols. Of course when I showed it to my children, they all had to try blowing it. To my two sons' dismay, only their sister could get it to make any sound at all.

My trip was over, but my memories were never-ending. And now a simple thank you didn't seem enough. Perhaps I could start a scholarship fund to send one of the Nakanais to school in Australia. That way, what might have seemed just a sentimental journey could have a lasting purpose. Little did I realize that the idea of a scholarship would turn into a school with an enrollment of nearly five hundred students by 1996.

A SCHOOL IS BORN

Back home, I wondered how I could repay the huge debt I owed to the friends who had saved my life. Fred Scherle, a Lutheran missionary home on leave from New Guinea, suggested building a school for the children of the village. At first, considering the cost, this seemed out of the question. But the more I thought about it, the more it made sense—not just scholarships for a few, but a school for all.

How would I go about raising the money? I realized I couldn't do it alone. There would have to be a committee or council of several, and we would need to establish a nonprofit foundation in order to solicit tax-exempt gifts. Les Mikeworth, a White Bear Lake attorney, drew up the application, but the IRS district office in St. Paul found all sorts of excuses for delaying action. At Les' suggestion I approached Senator Hubert Humphrey for help, and one of his staff arranged an appointment for me with the appropriate IRS department in Washington, DC.

The receptionist ushered me into a big conference room where I met three government attorneys seated at a long mahogany table. I started to tell them the circumstances that had led up to the project. When I mentioned New Guinea, one of the attorneys said he had flown a B-25 bomber there on combat missions during World War II. For the next twenty minutes the conversation centered on our war experiences. Finally one of the other attorneys broke in to ask why I had requested the meeting. Five minutes later I had verbal approval of our application to qualify as a 501(c-3) tax-exempt entity.

Back in White Bear Lake I started making the rounds of churches and service organizations, seeking financial help for the project. I also sent appeals to all my relatives (you learn a lot about your kinfolk in a situation like that).

And one weekend, at the invitation of Chester Franz, whom I had met through ham radio, I traveled to St. Louis to speak to three hundred members of the Rotary Club. Then the next day Chet flew me in a tiny Cessna airplane down to West Plains, Missouri, where I shared my story with twenty Rotarians there.

A series of articles in the *Minneapolis Tribune* sparked more interest—and our foundation's bank account began to grow. Then an article in the *Saturday Evening Post* brought responses from all across the country. A ninety-year-old woman from Connecticut sent a check in memory of her son, who had been killed in New Guinea. The women in a prayer circle in a tiny town in western Oklahoma sent their collection of three dollars and eighty-five cents.

Help kept coming. One day, on a plane ride from Atlanta to Minnesota, I sat next to an elderly woman from Minneapolis. Somehow our conversation turned to New Guinea and my dream of building a school for the people who had saved my life. A week later a check for five hundred dollars arrived in the mail with best wishes for success. By the spring of 1963 we had collected nearly fifteen thousand dollars.

In 1963 our son Dick graduated from White Bear Lake High. We had no intention of giving him a car as a graduation gift, but instead offered him a trip to a third-world country. If he wanted, he could accompany me to New Guinea to build classrooms for the Airmen's Memorial School at Ewasse, New Britain—about thirty miles east of Nantabu. (We decided against establishing the school in Nantabu because it lacked a flat building site, had only thirteen children living in it, and was very inaccessible to students from other areas. Soon afterwards, however, we built another school in Noau, which is very close to Nantabu.) I had arranged to hitch a ride on a C-54 transport plane from Travis Air Force Base (in California) with the 1,370th Mapping Group headed for Port Moresby.

Dick agreed to go. Since air force regulations kept him from traveling on a military aircraft, I dropped him off at San Francisco International to catch a Qantas 707 jet headed for Sydney, Australia. It was his first trip outside the continental United States. The next day, June 16, 1963, I met Captain Ed McGlinchy, the aircraft commander of the Douglas C-54. Except for Ed, the crew was not made up of what you might call "old hands." His co-pilot, who had been trained as a helicopter pilot, had just been recalled to active duty. The navigator, fresh from navigation school, was on his first trip over water. They call it OJT—on-the-job training. I checked out a parachute from operations and climbed aboard. The commander got on the microphone to brief us on ditching procedures. "The warning bell will ring for two or three seconds before an actual abort. Stay seated until after the third bounce." Comforting words to be sure.

It was sort of like a camping trip. A minivan brought out box lunches, a cooler filled with frozen dinners, a case of pint-sized cartons of milk, and enough coffee for a party of fifty. The weather officer forecast a fourteen-hour flight to Hawaii.

About ten minutes after we finally got airborne (much later than expected), the number-one engine started throwing oil across the wing. We had just barely reached the Golden Gate Bridge! The pilot did a one-eighty back to Travis, where we discovered the problem was caused by a loose connector on the hydraulic line that fed the prop-pitch control.

At this time I learned why we had failed to get off the ground on the original morning schedule. One of the exhaust stacks had a deep crack and had to be replaced. Now we were held up for another hour to change a servo unit on the radar because it would not sweep in search mode. I was beginning to wonder if hitching a ride on this tired old warhorse was such a good idea.

Because of the extended delays, the captain had to file a new flight plan. Finally, at five-thirty in the afternoon, we roared down the runway and were airborne—but not out of the woods. About an hour and a half out of San Francisco, the Loran navigation system went sour. The spare replacement module lasted about thirty minutes before it also failed, creating extra stress for our neophyte navigation officer.

The captain told the engineer to keep a close watch on engine oil consumption. We were using about one gallon per hour. Apparently this was not serious: they considered it cheaper to burn extra oil than to rebuild the engine.

It was a happy moment when we sighted the big island. Our wheels touched down at Hickam Field at six in the morning. After fourteen hours and ten minutes, I'm sure the engines were just as happy to quit as we were. Then, while moving along the taxiway over to the transient aircraft parking ramp, the number-two engine began to cough and clank like a bunch of tin cans bouncing behind a honeymoon car. Later our engineer found that a sparkplug had blown right out of the cylinder head. He also discovered the reason for the unusual loss of engine oil: a nut on one of the rocker arms had come loose and pierced a hole in the rocker cover. Since regulations limited the number of hours a crew could fly in any single twenty-four-hour period, we were obliged to spend the night in Hawaii.

Repairs were completed by early morning. All systems and engines checked OK. After topping off the fuel tanks and picking up food and soft drinks at the PX, we got back in the air and headed for Wake Island, our next refueling stop.

At 0130 GMT (Greenwich mean time) our navigator announced that we were crossing the International Date Line. In a flash I grew a day older as Tuesday became Wednesday. We arrived at tiny Wake Island at 3 P.M. local time.

We were off at nine the next morning with nothing but more water between us and Guam, our next stop. Anderson Field at the north end of the island rests on top of a cliff rising seven hundred feet out of the sea. With winds gusting in all directions, landings can be tricky. The air-conditioned rooms at the BOQ (bachelor officers' quarters) were especially welcomed. Each had a refrigerator filled with plenty of beer and soft drinks.

We were thankful to be on the last leg of our journey. Wake-up call came at two in the morning, and we stumbled through the dark for breakfast in the mess hall. Ten civilians were added to our passenger list. They were bound for Port Moresby to join a Navy LST (tank landing ship) on a mapping mission. I thought I might have the thrill of flying to New Guinea in a B-50 version of the B-29, but at the last minute several drums of JP-4 jet fuel were loaded into the belly. Passengers were not allowed to be on a plane carrying jet fuel as cargo.

We finally got in the air at six, about two thousand pounds heavier than usual. Our flight to Port Moresby was scheduled to take ten hours. We passed over Finschhafen on the north coast of New Guinea at twelve-thirty. Heavy cumulus clouds covered the Owen Stanley Mountains, so our pilot elected to fly down to Kiriwena and cross over the mainland at three thousand feet instead of going through Kokoda Pass at twelve thousand feet. This extra distance added another hour of flying time.

Dick was waiting when we touched down at Jackson Airport in Port Moresby. He had arrived two days earlier on a commercial airliner. I had been concerned about his welfare, but Keith McCarthy, Director of Native Affairs in New Guinea, had looked after him. I was most grateful for his kindness. The customs and immigration officers passed us through without delay and we took a taxi to the Papuan Hotel, which twenty years earlier had been headquarters for the Fifth Air Force bomber command. After a welcome bath we dropped in at the bar for a beer. What a small world! Sitting next to us was Walt Hocking, who had once lived in my hometown of White Bear Lake, Minnesota. We had never met, but it turned out he had sung in the choir where I went to church.

On Saturday we went into the TAA office to get our plane tickets to Rabaul. What an exercise that was. The airline calculates ticket prices in Australian dollars, but we were paying with U.S. travelers' checks. Since the exchange rate varies a fraction of a penny from day to day, our tickets could not be issued until the agent got the current rate from the local bank. It didn't open until ten, so we just sat.

At ten-thirty, tickets in hand, we finally went down to the harbor to meet Walt Hocking for a tour of the LST *Harris County*, which was being used to support a mapping mission. I had no idea that an LST was so big. A helicopter pad was installed on the afterdeck!

After lunching in the wardroom we returned to the hotel to meet June Kaad, wife of District Commissioner Freddie Kaad. Our transport was his official car. Mrs. Kaad asked the driver to take us to the Bomana War Cemetery, but a misunderstanding took us to the jail instead. It was enormous—and surrounded by beautiful gardens. Alice Collis, wife of the officer-in-charge, had created her own private zoo there, with deer, goats, and many exotic birds.

That afternoon Keith McCarthy, who had escaped from New Britain as the Japanese arrived, took us to his home for tea. His charming wife Jean told us that she had been the first white woman to visit the Nakanai area of New Britain where we planned to build a school. Keith was writing a book called *Patrol Into Yesterday*, which was published that fall. He held us spellbound with stories about his pre-war experiences in the bush.

Early Sunday morning Balfour "Bunny" Ogilvy picked us up at the hotel to drive us to the airport. Bunny was commodore at the local yacht club and a real character. He made a detour to the Papua Yacht Club to toss back "one for the road." According to him, a shot of whisky was a pre-flight requisite in New Guinea.

After an hour's wait at the airport, our DC-6 came limping in from Australia with one engine out. All of the passengers and baggage had to be transferred to a twin-engine DC-3, the only other aircraft available for the trip to Lae. A holdover from World War II, it still sported the cargo-style interior. Canvas webbed seats lined each side of the cabin, and the center aisle was piled high with cargo, an aluminum boat, and stacks of Sunday newspapers from Brisbane.

We made it to Lae and flew off to Rabaul the next morning. Matt Foley, ex-Coastwatcher with Ian Skinner's team, greeted us at the airport. We booked in at the Cosmo Annex, an extension of the Cosmopolitan Hotel overlooking Simpson Harbor. By U.S. standards the annex was a rather primitive accommodation. Mosquito netting enshrouded the beds, paper-thin walls allowed the slightest whispers to be heard in adjacent rooms, and a community shower with toilet facilities stood outside on a path leading from the annex to the main building. The waiters in the dining room did not speak English, so each item on the menu had a number assigned to it. Call out the wrong number and you might get fish instead of orange juice!

We had arrived at an important time in New Guinea's history. Until 1963 it was illegal for the natives to purchase alcoholic beverages. When the House of Assembly voted to end this restriction, even the church authorities had to lend support: they could not justify this blatant double standard. Since the ban was lifted on the day we arrived in Rabaul, a boisterous barroom at the hotel kept us awake most of the night.

The next day local news correspondent Gus Smales made plans for us to visit the Duke of York Islands in hopes of finding Ida. Our transport was a fifty-foot workboat filled with eight tons of assorted cargo that included cement, bags of rice, cases of tinned meat, and spare parts for plantation machinery. The skipper was a Tolai from Rabaul. Mount Matupi was putting on a show: puffs of steam were shooting up from her crater as we headed out of the harbor.

After two hours of pitching and rolling along at seven knots, we pulled into the wharf at Ullu, the Methodist coconut plantation. The manager was a young New Zealander. He and his wife drove us (in their World War II jeep) to the mission station to meet Ida and her family. I gave Ida a few gifts, including fabric for blouses, and arranged for her to pick up a big bag of rice at the mission trade store. Since she spoke no Pidgin, I could only wonder if she was remembering, as I was, her priceless gift to me twenty years earlier.

A short time later the jeep reappeared, loaded with new passengers anxious to get on the boat for the return trip to Rabaul. One woman carried a sick child who needed medical attention at the hospital there. I squeezed into the back seat between *lapuns* (senior citizens) and a bunch of cooking pots and bedding. There was no room for Dick, so he stood on the rear bumper and clung precariously to the frame for support. I remembered doing the same thing as a boy.

We spent the next few days with Herman Rothmier, the contractor we had hired to build our classrooms. Bert Price, a local welder, fabricated the roof supports out of two-inch steel water pipe. We needed to get all our building supplies to Ewasse, but discovered that shipping space was hard to find. A month earlier the six-hundred-ton *Pollurian* had capsized in a storm and gone to the bottom. Another ship, the *Kilinilau*, wound up on a mud bank in the Sepik, and the *Matoko* hit a reef. As a result the only ship available was the *Piri*, a decrepit old pre-war coastal vessel that had seen much better days. The skipper was anxious to go out with the tide around midnight. Matt Foley came down to the wharf to supervise the loading. Fluent in Pidgin, he soon had things under control. One of our fellow passengers was Marg Blake. She was taking a hundred newborn chicks to her plantation at Lolobau Island, which was just a couple of miles from the spot where I was shot out of the sky. Shortly after midnight the lines were cast loose and we headed out to sea. Cabin space was limited so Dick and I slept on the open deck.

We reached the Lolobau anchorage, 119 nautical miles from Rabaul, at five in the afternoon. Marg's husband Charlie met us with a dinghy to ferry their cargo ashore. Darkness came before we finished and the captain decided to remain overnight. The Blakes kindly invited Dick and me to join them for dinner at the plantation.

The boat's crew was aroused at first light to finish unloading. Dick and I went ashore to have a look at the Blake's radio transmitter, which had been giving them trouble. A faulty output meter made it impossible to properly tune the transmitter for maximum output. I placed a light bulb in series with the antenna and we got a good tune-up. Charlie was greatly pleased when the operator on the nine o'clock out-station schedule told us that the Lolobau signal was the strongest it had ever been. Their radio was a vital link to the outside world: that's how they ordered groceries and supplies from Rabaul, called for a medical charter in case of an emergency, and listened in on other conversations in order to catch up on the island news.

Our departure was delayed while the crew pumped diesel fuel from the ship's bulk tank into forty-gallon drums to be ferried ashore in a small boat. We finally got underway about one-thirty in the afternoon. We headed down the coast, threading our way at reduced speed through the treacherous reefs that border the shoreline. Three hours later we dropped anchor a couple of hundred yards offshore from Bialla, a coconut and cocoa plantation on the edge of Ewasse.

Eddie Tull, the plantation manager, came out in a motorboat to greet us. We could see a mob of people lining the shore. A group gathered at the end of the jetty and broke into song as we pulled alongside. There must have been over a hundred villagers waiting to greet us. Word had reached them by radio that we were coming to build a school. An archway of palm fronds, cockscomb, and hibiscus stretched across the end of the jetty. Choirs from several different villages took turns serenading us, and afterwards the people from Apupul placed gifts of food in a pile where Dick and I stood shaking hands. The reception line never seemed to end. I recognized the pattern from my previous visit to the area: the children obviously thought it was great fun to shake our hands and then go back to the end of the line for another pass.

Two chairs had been placed in a tractor-drawn trailer. We climbed aboard and took our seats of honor, feeling like the grand marshals of a parade. The only thing missing was a band playing "Pomp and Circumstance."

At Ewasse we were introduced to what would be our home for the next two weeks. Fashioned of bush materials for a native missionary, it rested on stilts about three feet off the ground. It had two bedrooms, a living room, and two small storerooms. Our toilet was a deep pit hidden back in the bush. A large canvas water bag with a spray nozzle at the bottom was our shower. The kitchen was a bush-material shed sitting off to one side of the main house.

The roof of our new home was covered with sacsac palm fronds, which provided food and shelter for the many tiny bugs that feasted twenty-four hours a day. Their droppings fell from the ceiling like rain. The floors were made from three-inch-wide strips of eucalyptus bark covered with newly woven reed mats. Cracks in the floors served as convenient ashtrays and good places to stub your toes. The whole place was gaily decorated in our honor with streamers of palm fronds and colored leaves.

After a supper of bully beef and rice, the village choir serenaded us and Luluai Peni gave a welcoming speech in Pidgin.

At six the next morning a bell signaled the morning prayer service. Then after breakfast we walked to Bialla and found that all of the cement, nails, and other supplies had been off-loaded and safely stored in a *copra* (coconut meat) shed.

On Saturday Dick and I were up early and off with a party of locals to search for a source of sand and gravel. We needed about sixty cubic yards to make cement floors for the classrooms. The beaches of New Britain are covered with fine black sand from volcanic outpourings, but the high salt content makes it unsuitable for cement. Fortunately, we found a fairly good supply of usable sand and gravel in a dried-up riverbed about a mile and a half from the building site. But we knew that moving it to the school could be a problem.

Sunday dawned bright and clear. The air was fresh from a light rain. When the bell (an empty World War II shell casing hanging from a tree) rang for the early worship service, the luluai brought us some bananas. Apmeledi, our faithful cook, served us smoked scrambled eggs and fresh bread with jelly. The local pastor, Eramus To Luaina, came over with his alarm clock so we could *mekim taim tru* (set the exact time). He explained the bell signals. First bell: *waswas taim* (time to take a shower); second bell: *putim an bilas* (get dressed); and third bell: *ol boi i go insait long haus lotu* (everyone go inside the church).

At the third bell Pastor Luaina came by to escort us to church. He was neatly dressed in a white shirt, white laplap, and dark tie. Apmeledi loaned us his prayer book, *A Buk Na Tinir*, and the hymnal, *A Buk Na Kakaila*. The congregation was already seated when Dick and I entered the church with the pastor. The pews were made of logs supported at the ends by forked sticks stuck in the ground. Chickens browsed across the dirt floor searching for scraps of food, and a Carnation milk tin holding a bouquet of artificial flowers sat on the altar. The pastor led us to a small wooden bench. First a Bible lesson was read in Maututu. Next a catechist delivered his sermon in rapid-fire bursts of Pidgin. (This was done for my benefit, but the words came too quickly for me to comprehend.) Then Pastor Luaina followed up with his sermon, once more in Maututu. I didn't understand a single word. At the conclusion the pastor, speaking in Pidgin, offered a thanksgiving to God for sending Dick and me to build them a school.

That night we became acquainted with creepy-legged strangers skittering up and down the walls of our bedroom. I guess they were attracted to the brilliant light of the gas lamp. One spider measured at least three inches from tip to tip. Another visitor was the rhinoceros beetle. Fortunately this amazing creature does not use its two big pincers to attack humans—but it *can* destroy a coconut tree!

On Monday Dick organized a group of fifty or sixty villagers equipped with heavy machete knives to finish clearing the area where the classrooms would stand. They moved across the ground with blades flying like a huge lawn mower. In the meantime I gathered a big group of women and children to haul sand. The women balanced pots and pans full of it on their heads, while the children carried it in coconut shells. It was mind-boggling to see such an ancient society only a one-day jet ride away from industrial America.

I was a bit concerned about the grave of a native missionary located in the middle of the school site. We were told that he had been "planted" in a wooden box and then covered over with a slab of concrete so wild animals wouldn't disturb him.

The classrooms were to be simple structures made from two-inch pipe welded into overhead trusses. David, our native carpenter, and his helper were busy making forms for the concrete piers that would support the pipes. The roofs would be made of corrugated iron, and the walls of eight-by-ten-foot sheets of Masonite.

The Tulls invited us for dinner again. Their generous hospitality was becoming an embarrassment. Ships that brought fresh meat and produce were few and far between. It didn't seem fair for casual visitors to be cutting so deeply into their short supply.

On Wednesday Dick went with a team of thirty natives to build a road that would enable the tractor and trailer to reach the sand and gravel pit at the creek. Eddie Tull realized that hauling sand and rock a mile and half with dishpans and copra bags would keep us and the crew busy until the next frost. He uncovered an old logging trailer that had not been used for five years, and in short order the native carpenters had built a flatbed capable of handling about ten tons of material on each trip.

On Thursday Father Wagner, a Catholic priest from Silanga, arrived to see what was going on. The jungle drums had been beating out stories of the project. Because he sported a foot-long goatee, he was known in Rabaul and Port Moresby as the "hippie priest."

The next morning Father Wagner returned to Silanga while Dick and I spent the day hauling sand. In the evening children from the village serenaded us with songs and presented us with several small shields painted in bright colors and festooned with chicken feathers. We discovered later that U.S. customs would not allow us to take these gifts home unless the feathers were removed.

A week later Dick and I headed back to White Bear Lake, leaving the contractor to finish building the school.

The following March the Airmen's Memorial School opened with four classrooms, four native teachers, an Australian headmaster named Jim Bye, and about forty first-through-fourth-grade students who studied English, arithmetic, and penmanship—plus social science, which was an exploration of the traditions, mythology, and oral history of their own culture. They even had a school garden.

A few months later Dorothy and I experienced the thrill of attending the school's official opening ceremony. Special orders issued by the war department covered our transportation to Sydney. The air attaché in the U.S. Embassy at Canberra arranged for the ambassador's DC-3 to fly us to New Guinea. Because of the plane's limited cruising range, we had to refuel and stay overnight at the RAAF Air Base in Townsville. At the Officer's Club that evening, we met some U.S. Navy pilots on temporary duty for a joint training exercise with the RAAF. When we told them the reason for our trip, they offered to do a flyover at the school. Two days later their twin-engine jet delighted the gathering with a low-altitude pass just as I delivered my speech.

TEACHING

Was my 1969 encounter with Minneapolis special-ed teacher Linda Parfrey just happenstance, or was it part of a divine plan that started with my survival in the jungle? For lack of anything better to do one night, she and a friend came to a prayer study group where I was sharing my World War II experiences and seeking support for the school. I had realized that recruiting good teachers was just as important as raising money, so I mentioned our desperate need for volunteers. The next morning Linda called to say that she and her husband Charlie might be interested.

Around the same time, word of the school's need for qualified teachers also reached the ears of Anne Huenemann, an idealistic and compassionate student at Macalister College in St. Paul, Minnesota. She was scheduled to marry classmate Jerry Parks right after graduation ceremonies in June. When she called Jerry to tell him about her "dream honeymoon" in the South Pacific, he thought she had lost her mind. But Anne won, and in July they climbed aboard a Qantas jet. Ten days later they were holding forth in classrooms at the Airmen's Memorial School on the island of New Britain, eight thousand miles from St. Paul.

Linda and Charlie arrived the following year. A talented musician, Linda not only taught the third grade but also trained the children's voices into a first-class choir. Charlie served as the school's handyman and entertained the kids with his guitar.

Meanwhile, UNIVAC granted me a one-year leave of absence so I could go to New Britain myself. I wanted to teach at the school as the climax of my longstanding desire to say thank you in a meaningful way. Dorothy was diabetic and the nearest medical help would be three days away by dugout canoe or two hours by charter aircraft—but she wanted to join me anyway, and got permission from her doctor to make the trip.

Armed with visas, immunization shots, and insulin, we boarded a Danish freighter at San Pedro, California. We were looking forward to an adventurous island-hopping trip across the Pacific. I brought my ham radio along so we could keep in touch with our families back in Minnesota. On our first night out, the captain opened his sailing orders and informed us that our next stop would be Brisbane, Australia. So much for island hopping. Our only sight of land during the entire sixteen days was a brief glimpse of the Fiji Islands.

In Sydney we were met by Air Vice-Marshall Bill Townsend and his wife Ruth. Bill had arranged passage on a RAAF plane from Sydney to Rabaul. I told him we were carrying quite a few personal things—including my ham radio equipment—and hoped the aircraft would have room for it all. "No worries," he said. "We'll be flying in a Lockheed C-130. It can hold fifteen tons of cargo." As operations officer for the RAAF, Bill had scheduled his annual inspection tour of Papua New Guinea to coincide with our trip.

As we approached Port Moresby, I was invited to the flight deck to sit in the co-pilot's seat. The captain disengaged the auto-pilot so I could get the feel of the huge bird in flight. I gingerly banked it into a gentle turn and was thrilled with its response to the controls.

We overnighted in Port Moresby and set out early the next morning for Rabaul. Since the airstrip at Bialla was not long enough for the big C-130, we shifted our cargo to the smaller twin-engine Caribou. As we lifted off on the final leg of our trip, I took Dorothy's hand in mine. Together we would see the culmination of my dream. My heart was full.

When we arrived at Ewasse in October of 1970, the school had grown to six grades with well over two hundred students, seven teachers (including Rick Chandler, an outstanding volunteer from Australia), and a wonderful native headmaster from New Ireland named Emil Nangsia. To make a long story very short, Dorothy and I ended up staying for four years! (Please see Appendix II at the back of the book for a glimpse into what our lives were like during that time.)

In June of 1974 we departed for home via Port Moresby and Sydney. Our years with the extraordinary people of New Guinea were rewarding for both of us. We were leaving what had come to be a second home, and I didn't know when or if I would ever return. When we got back to Minnesota, a friend asked if I thought I had repaid my debt. My eyes misted as I shook my head and replied, "I don't think I can ever pay for my life."

Many times over the years I've been asked if the Nakanai people have profited from the opportunity to learn at the Airmen's Memorial Schools. As with any cross-section of humanity, no matter where on the planet they live, some have been inspired to go on to higher education and have done marvelously well, while others have learned what they needed to survive and thrive in their ever-developing society.

The most prominent of our graduates is Garua Peni. Like virtually all of our students, she couldn't speak a word of English when she started school. By the time she was in the sixth grade, she dreamed of being a teacher. Today she holds a master's degree in linguistics from the University of Sydney, and is a professor at the University of Papua New Guinea.

Two of our students have become attorneys in Port Moresby, and several others are in nursing. And of course the most exciting result (for me at least) is the fact that three of our graduates—Dorcas Saua, Joseph Taboga, and Paul Pius—are now on the teaching staff in Ewasse.

THE ADVENTURE CONTINUES

After four years in the heat of the tropics, Dorothy and I decided that the cold Minnesota winters were not for us. My sister Mary Louise owned several acres in the Sierra Nevada foothills near Grass Valley, California, so when I retired from UNIVAC in 1978, we moved there and rented a small home from her. In 1981 we joined with her to run a five-acre vineyard. (I wanted to plant blueberries, but Mary Lou, who was a big fan of the *Falconcrest* television series, decided it just had to be grapes.) Our Zinfandel won several awards in Nevada County, but finally the nurturing, pruning, and harvesting of twenty-five hundred vines got to be more than our aging bodies could handle. In 1995 we sold the vineyard to Phil and Anne Star, which gave me more time for volunteer work. Before long I found my niche at Hennessy School in Grass Valley— as a mentor in the second- and third-grade classes of Melissa Fowlkes and Grace Dolan.

Then in 1999, fifty-four years after my plane went down in the jungle, I finally learned why the Japanese pilot had spared my life. I had always wanted to meet him, because in essence it was his gun that planted the seed that eventually grew into the school that fell from the sky. A friend led me to Los Angeles history buff Henry Sakaido, who led me to Japanese historian Kazuhiko Osuo, who led me to Mitsugu Hyakutomi of Yamaguchi-ken, Japan. Mitsugu was flying a Nishiki-fukusen (a double-engine Ki-45 fighter plane) for the Japanese Imperial Army's 13th Air Group when he shot down a P-38 over New Britain in June of 1943.

By the time I found Mitsugu he was too ill with Alzheimer's to speak with me, but his wife Teruko answered my letter. She wrote that although her husband rarely talked about World War II, he did say that he could never bring himself to shoot helpless enemy pilots hanging from their parachutes! So at last I knew the whole story.

A year later, in the spring of 2000, I returned to Papua New Guinea for what I believed would be my last visit. (Of course, I had experienced that very same feeling on eight earlier visits.) But this time a noteworthy surprise greeted me.

On May 8, one day after my eighty-fourth birthday, the Nakanai people crowned me *Suara Auru* (chief warrior) in a special ceremony at the school in Ewes. They painted my face, decorated my arms and legs with bands and bracelets, and placed a regal headaddress upon my head. Garua Peni gave a moving speech, and then Elias Paraide, an elder from the village of Matililiu, presented me with a spear and a shield. Beautiful hymns and dances—including a traditional *piako* performed by young boys from Ewasse—completed the celebration.

It was so unexpected that I felt serenely numb! I also realized just how close my relationship with these beloved friends had become. Beautiful and luxurious as their country was, it was the people who kept bringing me back. I had found my purpose in life.

APPENDIX I

CONFIDENTIAL

SS212/A I6-3
Serial (04)

c/o Fleet Post Office
San Francisco, Calif.

7 February 1944

From: The Commanding Officer .
To: The Commander, Task Force Seventy-Two

SUBJECT

Report of Special Mission, February 3-6, 1944

In order that Task Force Commander may limit distribution of this report, it is submitted separately from the war patrol report covering the period.

OBJECT

To remove from Matanakunai, OPEN BAY, NEW BRITAIN, the Australian Coastwatcher and as many shot-down Allied aviators as could be assembled there. We were to conceal our presence until clear of the land, then disclose our presence by a lengthy radio transmission to give false impression that subs were patrolling that area.

NARRATIVE

3 February 1944

Escorted by PT 190 and PT 323 from DREGER HARBOR, NEW GUINEA, thru VITIAZ STRAIT.

1900 (L) Released escorts and set course for GAZELLE PENNINSULA.

4 February 1944

0329 (L) Submerged north of VITU ISLANDS for daylight run.

1951 (L) Surfaced at dark to approach coast.

2215 (L) In Lat. 04-22' S/Long. 130-50' E, a large flying boat crossed our bow in moonlight, distant 3 miles, altitude 600 ft. As plane turned toward us, GATO dived. No bombs were dropped.

2336 (L) In order to clear the spot before destroyers arrived from RABAUL, surfaced and stood toward OPEN BAY at best speed.

5 February 1944

Reconnoitered OPEN BAY to locate point designated for rescue. Submerged at dawn.

1100 (L) Distinguished white marker on shore. This was one of the signals suggested to the Coastwatcher.

1937 (L) Surfaced in trimmed-down condition 2 miles from designated landing point, headed in, all 20-mm and 80-cal weapons manned, sound gear and pitometer log housed. Propulsion by battery motors. Party on beach immediately flashed the proposed signal (by hand flashlight).

2010 (L) No enemy activity having been noted to seaward or landward, launched two rubber boats. As is customary, these were manned by selected volunteers (Lieut. John E. Gilman, Jr., USNR; Lt. James R. Swanbeck, USN; H.L. Storti, S1c, USN; D.M. Sly, S1c, USNR). The boats made the beach thru the surf without mishap.

2051 (L) The Coastwatcher and four aviators were quickly embarked in the boats, which then started the return. Having covered about 200 yards of the return journey, they heard a commotion on the beach. Some crude blinker signaling was being perpetrated. From GATO it read "Sixty-seven more aviators." We commenced breaking out our wooden boat for a ferry, and directed the cook to prepare soup for about eighty guests. Meantime the rubber boats returned to the beach. They found three additional aviators who, having been notified by native runner of the evacuation, had made forced marches from across NEW BRITAIN via jungle and mountain. They were embarked in the rubber boats.

2121 (L) Boats reached GATO. While guests were being given the Six-B treatment (bath, bandage, bread, butter, bullion, and bed), GATO extricated herself, transmitted the message, and then set out on four engines for VITIAZ STRAIT.

6 February 1944

Proceeding (submerged during daylight) towards rendezvous with PT boats.

0626 (L) Effected rendezvous with PT 192 and PT 326 at north end of VITIAZ STRAIT and proceed toward destination.

1350 (L) Entered DREGER HARBOR, P.N.G., and moored to U.S.S. PORTUNAS. Disembarked following passengers:

1. Wing Commander W. Townsend, C.C., 22nd Squadron R.A.A.F. (Shot down at PALMALMAL 11-3-43.)
2. Major A.W. Roberts, A.I.A.I.B. (Coastwatcher)
3. Capt. Fred Hargesheimer, A.C., U.S. Army. (Bailed out of P-38 near UBILI, 6-5-43.)
4. Lt. Edward J. Czarnecki A.C., U.S. Army. (Bailed out of P-38 near WIDE BAY, 10-23-43.)
5. Lt. Carl G. Planck, A.C., U.S. Army. (Crash-landed in water off TALILI Plantation, 11-2-43.)
6. Flying Officer D. McClymont, R.A.A.F. (Shot down over PALMALMAL, 11-3-43.)
7. Lt. O.M. Giertson, A.G., U.S. Army. (Crash-landed a P-38 8 miles off WIDE BAY, 11-2-43.)
8. Master Sgt. G.R. Manuel, bombardier of Flying Fortress

and its only survivor. (Bailed out 6 miles off PUTPUT
HARBOR, 5-21-43.)

R.J. FOLEY

APPENDIX II

Excerpts from Ewasse Journal
1971-1974

1 February 1971

Still no word from the new headmaster Alf Parrish. Sent a wire to the education department at Kimbe for instructions. Everyone spent the morning arranging books in the library, painting desks, etc. Women from the village came over to rake grass and tidy up the school grounds. At 11 A.M. we had our first successful radio contact with Minneapolis. Talked for over an hour to Bill Cuniff and Bill Higgins. Bankstown air service flew in a shiny new North Istaforder to demonstrate to the Complex Plantation. Rain started to fall at 1:30 P.M.

2 February 1971

Situation still desperate. No word on new headmaster or the third administrative teacher, Miss Nanani. Registration opened at 8 AM. School fee is $1, and P&C (Parents & Citizens Association) dues are $2. Charlie organized sports while Linda, Saimon Tatinia, and I enrolled the children. A flood of new students! Not knowing the policy on minimum starting age, I may have created a problem by accepting everyone born in 1964 or earlier. Sixteen new students were enrolled in Jim's Standard I class. If everyone shows, he will have 51 children! By noon 48 (about one-third of the student body) had enrolled—including one transfer student from Silanga.

Dorothy is working with two older girls to arrange the library. Cement mixer failed to show and building crew is mixing cement by hand for the foundation of residence #6. Lots of confusion during registration. Some children seem to have several names. P&C president Daniel August was most helpful—without him to interpret, all would have been lost.

3 February 1971

Continued hand-mixing concrete for house, a very slow process. Half the slab finished today. Villagers are developing a desire for eggs. Dorothy has a handshake price of 80 cents per dozen. No headmaster yet.

Survived another day in classroom. Several boys asked about vocational school. Parents are concerned about boys getting out of school and suddenly being *sindaun nating* (sitting down with nothing to do). Must give early attention to this problem.

6 February 1971

No headmaster yet. Dorothy and I are ready to climb the walls. Our new call letters are "VK9 Funny House." Had another excellent radio contact with Bill. Eric and Carol were there and we talked for an hour. Eighteen degrees in Minneapolis, with heavy snow. Weather here has been amazingly dry for the monsoon season—no real rain for the past ten days. Philip the cook from Complex came over for the evening and spent most of his time on ham radio. Had an amazing contact with John Keith.

9 February 1971

No headmaster yet. Charlie installed aerials for school broadcasts but program is apparently delayed until 15 February. Father Wagoner arrived in afternoon with gifts of wine and chocolate candy, plus rumors about changes in Department of Education. Several staff changes at HQ at Kimbe: Fred Liver resigned, and a man from the highlands has come in as inspector for our district. Robin Brown is new kiap (officer-in-charge) for Ewasse patrol post. Has requested enrollment of his daughter Margaret in Standard IV. Daniel August came to discuss students who were expelled from school several years ago. They have missed so much work that it's impossible to let them back in. Their parents will be upset, so we decided to advise them through the P&C council committee. No sooner had we finished the meeting than Iska and Tony Avenel from North Britain Electronic dropped by for the evening. We are finding it difficult to get our homework done with all the night visitors.

10 February, 1971

Started moving Jim Bye's personal effects. Three children have been getting daily treatment for grille (a fungal skin disease) from Tabita.

12 February, 1971

The school dugout canoe drifted out to sea during the night and was picked up by a Japanese logging ship. When the schoolboys went to retrieve it, they were told they would have to pay $10 because it had been abandoned. I sent a note to Complex demanding is return—otherwise they would have an "international incident" on their hands.

This morning I demonstrated the ham radio to five ex-schoolboys. Les Bell, the operator at the other end, was a perfect contact, having spent most of his life on a plantation in New Ireland. He spoke to all of the boys and helped make it exciting for them.

Hamburger, powdered mushroom soup, and a squirt of tomato juice made a delicious sauce to pour over spaghetti for dinner. Charlie came down at 8 P.M. for an evening on the radio, a great success. We began with an hour's conversation on the VK9 net to catch up on all the territory news. Gene Nurka, VK9GN, filled us in on the landslide tragedy near Telefomen, which took the lives of a couple from the Summer Institute of Linguistics and their two children. A small 500-foot mountain disintegrated and pushed huge trees and soil down the ravine a quarter of a mile to engulf an entire village. It was all over in twenty minutes. No one dreamed such a thing could happen. Later in the evening we had an exciting visit with KC6JC—Father Joe Cavanaugh, a Catholic priest at Ponopoe in the Eastern Caroline Islands. He has been working there since 1956 and finds the problems quite similar to the ones here, especially in teaching primary-age children. Two of his teachers are Peace Corps workers.

15 March 1971
More brown rice and split coconuts for the chickens. One of the villagers brought a two-year-old boy, Malagu Kau, who was suffering from what appeared to be pneumonia. We are desperate for the medical assistant. I had no choice but to send the child to Ian McPherson at Bialla—a tortuous journey on foot through mud and rain. Dorothy wrapped him in one of her sweaters to keep him warm.

7 April 1971
Rain started to fall at 3:30 this morning and continued throughout the day. *Twin Otter* dipped under the overcast, made two circles of the field, didn't like what it saw, and flew on to Rabaul. There was heavy absenteeism because of the rain—over two inches in about six hours, overflowing the tanks and making the roads impassable. I reverted to my childhood days and spent the morning cutting blouse patterns for school uniforms from the *Christian Science Monitor*. As

soon as we cut the first sample, Tabitha sewed it and then raced up for a trial fit on the children. But we had failed to allow extra material for seams, and they thought it a great joke when it wouldn't go over their heads. The instructions in *Garment Patterns by Simple Methods* (published in Australia in 1945) described the bodice pattern as "a plain foundation which may be converted into many useful garments." Unfortunately our bust and waist measurements were not sufficient , and on top of that our guess on the arm holes fell short, so after we connected the neckline the children couldn't get their arms into the sleeves. I'm sure we wouldn't have had all this trouble if Dort had let *me* take the measurements!!

8 April 1971

Our supply of laying pellets is being eaten up much faster than I expected. If the *Carla Mavas* doesn't come next week with a new supply, the girls in the hen house will be back on a diet of oatmeal and coconuts. The weather looks like a repeat of yesterday. A strong wind came up at 4 A.M. and we scurried around closing windows before the rain began to fall. We're praying for a letup so Allison Gough and her friend can get in on the *Twin Otter* flight from Rabaul, but right now, at 9 A.M., the outlook is doubtful.

Joe Moscov came down with a message that Father Wagoner wants us to come to Selanga for Easter, but I'm afraid we can't leave our chickens unattended—and it would be no fun in the rain. Off to the airstrip at 10 A.M. to meet Allison and Clair Fowler, arriving from Rabaul. After waiting around for an hour, Charlie came trudging up from headquarters to tell us that the airstrip had been closed and that no planes would be coming in today.

9 April 1971

The *Twin Otter* came flying over at 9:39 A.M. and we all made a mad dash for the strip. The passengers and cargo were discharged before we got there, so I met Allison and Claire, followed by a crowd of school children, walking up the road. Claire Fowler is a delightful girl—she used to work as an agricultural chemist and is now writing for the agriculture publications department. The plane brought some groceries but no mail—big disappointment for all. Apparently the post office in Rabaul is closed for a five-day holiday.

23 April 1971

Dorothy spent an uncomfortable night scratching sand fly bites. One of Linda's relatives sent her some Panalog ointment, an anti-fungal and anti-inflammatory agent sold only to veterinarians. We think that if it cures cows, it should help Dorothy. Will report later for the record. Linda claims it formed a scab on one of her open sores after only six hours.

27 June 1973

A date I'll never forget! For the past two weeks I've been filling in as the cook at a nearby logging camp. (The regular cook got mad at some of the employees and just packed his bags and left.) I arrived at the company mess to find that the electric power had been out since 6 A.M. due to a breakdown of the diesel engine. A hasty change in the menu received approval from the loggers.

Spent the afternoon on the tractor hauling cement blocks to the health centre. Then, as I was taking a shower, a motorcycle came roaring down the path and skidded to a halt at our front door. The native rider rushed up to report on an accident at the Oil Palm project. The sawmill roof had collapsed, killing a Japanese carpenter and injuring five others—four natives and one Japanese. A moment later Ken Yamoe drove up to ask for help getting a charter flight from Rabaul. For over an hour I tried desperately to make radio contact—without success.

At 5:30 P.M. I had to leave for the mess hall at the logging company to cook the evening meal. The first batch of fish in beer batter had just begun to crisp when Brian Dixie pulled up to advise that a mercy charter flight carrying a doctor from Rabaul was expected to land in twenty minutes. The Department of Civil Aviation (DCA) wanted me to keep watch on the VHF channel so I could talk to the pilot as he approached the area. I borrowed the Toyota and raced off to our house to fire up the radio. The sun had set and Dorothy had already left in our Datsun pickup to help light the airstrip.

Finally I was able to raise the aircraft, *Uniform November King*. I spoke to the pilot, Wren Fennimore, who was making his very first night flight in New Guinea. He was passing Sule and estimated his arrival at Bialla in fifteen minutes. Dort drove up to the house to find out if the pilot had any instructions for the ground crew.

By the time we got back to the airstrip, about twenty cars and trucks were parked alongside with headlights aimed across the strip per instructions from the DCA. Two petrol drums with flaming laplap wicks sticking out the top were placed at each end to guide the pilot to the first night landing in the airport's history.

After waiting 40 minutes we began to wonder if the pilot had gotten lost. Messengers kept running between the strip and the patrol-post HQ where radio contact was in progress with the DCA. I finally drove back to our house for another try at reaching the pilot on the VHF channel. At 8:30 P.M. I made contact. Wren reported in from 10,000 feet, somewhere near Kimbe about 50 miles to the south. He had overflown Bialla because the cloud cover had blocked our lights from view. The DME navigation system at Hoskins was inoperative and he would have to follow the shoreline back to us from Kimbe. He suggested that we listen for the sound of his engines and then alert him as to his position. We felt he would be too high for us to hear from any great distance, so we asked him to flash his landing lights. A few minutes later he reported seeing lights on the coast and asked me to stand by the radio until he made positive identification of his position. When he spotted the flaming torches at the end of the runway, he let me go back to the strip. He did a beautiful job on his first New Guinea night landing, bringing the plane to a stop before reaching the halfway point.

Wren's passenger was a young Aussie doctor who was also having his first-ever night flight in a light aircraft. Dorothy and I brought the most seriously injured patient to him in our Datsun pickup. After a thorough examination of all the patients, he decided that the situation did not warrant risking another night-flight back to Rabaul. The pilot stayed over with us while the doctor looked after his charges at the health centre. A cement mixer with an auxiliary power unit supplied them with electricity all night long.

28 June 1973
We were up at first light. A big crowd had already gathered at the health centre to watch the young doctor make his rounds. One of the Japanese staff arrived with hot tea, bread, and tined meat for the patients. The only person who required treatment at the hospital in Rabaul was one of the injured native carpenters (the doctor suspected a spinal injury).

At 7:15 A.M. another charter, the *Aztec*, arrived with Barry Morrow in the driver's seat. Wren and I picked him up at the strip and went into a huddle with the doctor to see who would go along on the trip to Rabaul. A total of ten passengers made up the final list:

- the injured native carpenter
- his *wantok* (friend from the same tribal area—comes from "one talk")
- a young boy from Baikakea suspected of having tetanus
- the boy's guardian
- Mr. Kawashima, managing director of the Oil Palm Company
- Ken Yazome, the interpreter
- the dead Japanese carpenter
- the doctor
- two pilots

In the meantime, a radio message reported that an RAAF Iroquois helicopter was in the area on a supply mission and would be taking on fuel at Ewasse. It landed at 8:30 A.M. To the great delight of the charter pilots, the helicopter crew offered to carry the dead body back to Rabaul. (The ventilation system of the helicopter is far superior to that of the plane's tiny cabin!)

Getting the seriously injured carpenter into the plane proved to be tricky since the *Aztec* lacks special accommodations for stretcher patients. We removed the rear seats, placed a thick mattress on the floor, and then pulled him on his blanket stretcher through the rear cargo hatch.

All aircraft were cleared from the airstrip by 9:15 A.M., just 20 minutes before the *Twin Otter* arrived on its regularly scheduled run.

Unfortunately, it turns out that Rabaul has no cremation facilities, so several hours later another charter brought the body back (stuffed in its rear cargo compartment). It was taken to the Oil Palm camp, which was put temporarily off-limits. Word quickly spread through the villages that the Japanese were going to *kukim* (cook) the body.

5 July 1973
Mr. Phil Chee arrived to take over my duties as chief cook at the logging camp. Visiting with him over a cup of coffee, I learned that he was born in Papua New Guinea, speaks fluent German, and has never worked as a professional cook—although apparently he brought some ancient Chinese herbs to enhance the flavors of his dishes.

24 July 1973
Roof tank went dry this morning. Tabitha washed clothes in the river. Attempts to repair generator from parts in the junk box were unsuccessful. I discovered that the cause of rectifier failure was a shorted capacitor used for field stabilization.

Michael Ogio, district education inspector, arrived on the *Ganua* for an advisory visit. The boat also brought a YWCA girls' baseball team from Hoskins for a game with Ewasse.

Dort took advantage of our electricity and water supply failures by having a warm bath at the McPherson's. Our teachers have become so dependent on electric lights that their kerosene lamps were covered with dust and not ready for the emergency. The power failure made them realize how fortunate they have been to have electric lights in their houses.

7 June 1974
Wage earners on the plantation have a custom called *Sande Pe*. Each fortnightly payday four or five *wantoks* join together in the scheme. One member collects all the pay—his own and everybody else's. Then on the next payday another member gets it all. This system serves as an equalizer because the member with the highest wage always ends up on the short end.

11 June 1974
Esoram Toligu, District Superintendent of Education, and Wai Wai Waterhaus, the new district education inspector, arrived unexpectedly on a charter flight from Hoskins. This sent Dort hustling to clear the debris from our guestroom, which had been serving as a storage space. It was the DS's first visit to our school. After observing classes all morning, we took a drive around the area. They told us that the plans for the new Oil Palm town site included 75 acres for education. We had a long discussion about the future of

124

the Airmen's Memorial School in view of the expected influx of settler families. Depending on the census results, we may need to add more classrooms.

14 June 1974

Bishop Gaius and Densuit Laviliu, United Church minister, dropped in for morning tea. We had a *toktok* about how we can help the people who looked after me during the war. They now realize that building a school in Nantabu is impractical because of the small number of children. I told them that Gabu had suggested a church or chapel as a memorial to Luluai Luau, the late chief. I agreed to discuss the idea further with Gabu, and also with Lauo's son Walu. We also might consider high-school scholarships for the Nantabu children.

Bishop Gaius sees no problem having the church office at Rabaul handle the school's financial affairs after I leave. Will contact their treasurer Bob Coulson to discuss details and prepare a budget.

16 June 1974

Lots of activity on the waterfront. We were awakened at 6 A.M. by the reverberations of the logging ship as it thumped out through the reefs guided by a tug boat. An hour later a parade of canoes appeared, loaded with visitors leftover from the church celebration at Matililiu.